Success-Speak

The Art of Maximizing Your Potential
Through What You Say

A Full Year of Inspiring Success Quotes from

Steven K. Dunn

THREE SKILLET

SUCCESS-SPEAK: THE ART OF MAXIMIZING YOUR POTENTIAL
THROUGH WHAT YOU SAY, ANNOTATED EDITION, Dunn, Steven K.

1st ed.

THREE SKILLET

www.ThreeSkilletPublishing.com

ISBN: 978-1-943189-52-6

— Introduction —

C. S. Lewis once said that a man can no more diminish God's glory by refusing to worship Him than a lunatic can put out the sun by scribbling the word "darkness" on the walls of his cell.

Finding success in everyday life is the same for many of us. People around us are constantly scribbling disparaging frowns, snide comments, and gut-busting criticisms on our attempts to rise above our circumstances.

We can escape their prison cells with *Success-Speak*. We can recharge our minds and bask in the sunlight of success by saying these three words: *I will succeed.*

Of course, it's more difficult than just saying three words, but that's a good place to start. Once we've internalized that concept, we can move on into specific areas of our life where we can begin to see results. Soon we'll keep the sink clean every day. We'll get dressed before we get the mail. We'll register for that college class, apply for that job; and we'll get there, even if we must beg a ride.

You see, success happens because we make it happen. No one in the prison cell of defeat has the right to tell us our success can't happen, all because they've written our future on the wall. Our future isn't in their hands. It's in ours.

This book gives you *Success-Speak* jump starters for every day of the year. Read them first thing in the morning to get your mind on how you are going to make your day successful. Then *write it down.* You're making a plan and setting a goal for the day. You are saying, "This is how I'm changing my life from this day forward. This is the new me, not the writing on yesterday's wall. My prison cell of defeat can't hold me any longer. I've left that building, the doors are locked, and I can't get back inside. I'm moving forward into my new life."

If you want to find success in your life, *Success-Speak* will help you get there. Your job is to take the first step with Day 1.

Let's get started.

Steven K. Dunn
Author of *Success-Speak: The Art of Maximizing Your Potential Through What You Say*

"If you don't shake off your doubts and forge a path forward through the veiled path of possibilities and unknowns before you, then you will never know what heights you can reach, the dreams you can accomplish, or the positive difference you can impart."

— Steven K. Dunn —

— Day 1 —

*"If you let your personal life, your family,
or your spirituality suffer to further
wealth or power, you have not been
successful."*

◀   *Romans 8:6*   ▶

*For to set the mind on the flesh is death, but to set the mind on the
Spirit is life and peace.*

Our faith in Christ flows from our belief in the sacrifice of Christ on the cross and the salvation message in His death and resurrection.

Christ's message to us is to enact a spiritual change in how we live our lives. If our focus is on money, houses, and cars, we've missed Jesus' mark.

Certainly, our Lord knows we need these things to survive, but they cannot be our focus. If all we care about is the size of our bank account, we may well lose everything else.

We must ask ourselves what we've given up achieving our success. Our personal standards? The people around us? Our spiritual connection with Christ?

We have one goal in life when we confess Christ as our Lord: to set our mind on the Spirit so we can find life and peace.

— Day 2 —

*"Even the greatest accomplishments in
our life are eclipsed by the glory of God.
Serve Him in all that you do."*

◀   *Philippians 2:13*   ▶

*For it is God who works in you, both to will and to work for his
good pleasure.*

The sun is a brilliant star that warms our earth.

Yet, in an eclipse, the moon easily covers the sun, and its
shining power becomes nothing.

It's easy for us to see our awards, our university degrees, and
our business accolades as the point of our lives. If we do, we've
burned bright and hot, yet everything we've done will be wasted.

Our lives in Christ need to be hidden behind what He desires
in us. However brightly we shine—and we should shine in
everything we desire to accomplish—we must see the work we
do in the Father as our crowning achievement.

The plans of our Lord will eclipse those of humanity no
matter how we try to relegate Him to the periphery. When we
serve Him as our Lord and Savior, we'll be lifted up with Him,
and His light will shine through us.

— Day 3 —

"If you make an attempt and don't succeed, that is not a failure. All you've done is discovered one way not to proceed. Get up, learn from your experience, and make another attempt."

◀❙   2 *Corinthians* 12:9-10   ❙▶

But he said to me, "My grace is sufficient for you, for my power is made perfect in weakness." Therefore I will boast all the more gladly of my weaknesses, so that the power of Christ may rest upon me. For the sake of Christ, then, I am content with weaknesses, insults, hardships, persecutions, and calamities. For when I am weak, then I am strong.

The Apostle Paul grasped onto his weakness as his strength in the Lord. More so, he boasted of his weakness. It enthused the apostle to see Christ as his salvation and his strength, even in his failures.

Failing is giving up. That can never be our option. If the apostle had thrown up his hands in despair each time something bad happened in his life, modern Christendom would be missing a large portion of the New Testament.

Whatever our weaknesses are, our duty in Christ is to lay them on Him, to depend on our Lord to be there when we are weak, and to call upon Him to be our strength and our fortress.

— Day 4 —

"Nearly all of us know the pain that comes with being deceived. Yet even knowing that, are you still going to tell that lie?"

◀   *Psalm 101:7*   ▶

No one who practices deceit shall dwell in my house; no one who utters lies shall continue before my eyes.

"It was for your good."

We've all heard that, the lie having been told to make us feel better, or to hide something that someone didn't want us to know. It may have worked for a time, but then the lie came to light.

The dishonesty was exposed. Oh, how our heart was pierced with the agony of the lie!

We can call it "white," a misrepresentation, or a simple fib. It all means the same thing. We intended to deceive someone. The truth was sidelined, kicked to the side, and for what purpose?

The Word of God assures us that "no one who practices deceit shall dwell in my house."

No one means no one, no matter how good our intentions.

— Day 5 —

"If you cannot stand by your actions without feeling ashamed, then the time to change is now."

Isaiah 50:7   I▶

But the Lord GOD helps me; therefore I have not been disgraced; therefore I have set my face like a flint, and I know that I shall not be put to shame.

Mistakes come easily to most of us.

We stumble, and when we climb to our feet, we're soiled with the evidence of our fall. Our reputations are stained. Our relationships are tattered. Our job is in peril.

All we can do is move forward. God assures us that with His help, we will not be disgraced. He will cover us with new robes, repair our damaged reputations, and mend our relationships.

The crux of our change comes in us. We must modify what we've been doing. Behave differently. Speak differently. Model our lives after the example of our Lord.

It takes determination. We must "set our face like a flint," that we might find the strength to follow in the footsteps of the righteous. The Lord will empower us in our time of need.

— Day 6 —

"If you want success, you can achieve it."

◄   *Philippians 4:13*   ▮►

I can do all things through him who strengthens me.

The American work ethic is one of being able to achieve anything we want.

No matter where we start out, we can be the master of anything we choose.

Our job? We can be the head of the company.

Our personal life? Our vacations and leisure time can take us around the globe.

In politics? Governor or President isn't too much to ask.

Our first step is to depend on the strength of the Lord. When we look to Him as the author and the finisher of our faith, then we have the foundation for success, both spiritually and financially.

We can change the world around us, when we build our relationship with our Lord. He gives strength to all who ask.

— Day 7 —

"Success is not something that comes without significant work."

◀︎ *Colossians 3:23* ▶︎

Whatever you do, work heartily, as for the Lord and not for men.

Winning the lottery is a dream of unimaginable luxury for many people.

Just to imagine more money than we can possibly spend sends jitters up and down our spine.

Yet, what happens to most lottery winners? Within a decade, the money is gone, and there's nothing left.

It's the financial and mental discipline we learn through years of striving to be successful that gives us a grasp on the real world. An entrepreneur can strike it big through a chance success, but without putting in the hours to ensure his investments, he risks having his success evaporate before his eyes.

We can't rest on our past triumphs. We must strive to move forward, to work as for the Lord. When we break a sweat in achieving what we want, we'll find our victory at the end of each day.

— Day 8 —

"Holding grudges will hold you back in life."

◀   Leviticus 19:18   ▶

You shall not take vengeance or bear a grudge against the sons of your own people, but you shall love your neighbor as yourself: I am the LORD.

Grudges are like tar balls. Once we pick them up, they stain us for a very long time.

The stain also rubs off on everything we touch, from our clothes, to the people we hug, to the surfaces in our cars and homes.

It makes a mess for others to clean up.

The only way to deal with grudges is to walk away from them. Never pick them up. And if we do? Get rid of them as quickly as possible and scrub away the residue until it's all shiny and clean.

The residue of a grudge is scoured away by the effects of love. A soft voice, kind words, and treating others well can polish away the grime of our grudge.

— Day 9 —

"If you truly want to achieve your goal, to live your dreams, you will not let anything stand in your path."

◄| *Ephesians 3:20* |►

Now to him who is able to do far more abundantly than all that we ask or think, according to the power at work within us . . .

A path can go uphill or downhill. It can wander along the edge of the shore or twist through a forest preserve. Sometimes we can see past the next curve, and other times, the view ahead is blocked by trees, hills, or debris.

We don't stop walking just because we can't see where we're going.

If a storm comes though and a branch blocks our path, we climb over it, because we can see that the path continues on the other side.

Our goals in life are the same. We must continue to pursue them despite financial disasters, relationship catastrophes, and emotional pitfalls. Success-speak can provide us motivation.

Just because the branch is in our path is no reason to give up on our destination. God will lead us toward our goal.

— Day 10 —

"Remember that success rarely falls into your lap. You must make the conscious decision to succeed before success can be yours."

◀   Proverbs 15:22   ▶

Without counsel plans fail, but with many advisers they succeed.

A solitary tree can't become a forest, no matter how hard it tries.

That may seem silly to us, but how many people try to become successful without the proper preparation?

We need people to aid us in deciding our future, to help us formulate our plans, and to steer us away from certain disaster.

It's hard work to be successful. Don't let anyone suggest otherwise. That musician that explodes on the scene? How many years did she play the small venues? Financial wizards often start out barely getting by, making small investments, until the big payoffs begin to come in.

Today's verse says that "with many advisers they succeed." To reach your success, find a mentor, a counselor, someone to give you advice. Then act. Move out. Success is yours to earn, but you do have to earn it.

— Day 11 —

"A single action can resonate throughout your entire life, whether it be negative or positive."

◀   *James 1:25*   ▶

But the one who looks into the perfect law, the law of liberty, and perseveres, being no hearer who forgets but a doer who acts, he will be blessed in his doing.

A teenager has an inattentive moment, loses control of the car, and four people die.

It happened near Fredericksburg, Texas, in 2016. One moment, and the world changed for three families.

A man gives up His life on a cross, offering His blood as salvation for the innocent, and millions of people are saved.

It happened on Golgotha two millennia ago.

Our opportunity for good is now. One action, then another, and another. When we live out the Word of God in all that we say and do, we become a force for good in the world.

The choice is ours. Be inattentive and watch people die, or live by the standards of the Lord so that others may live.

— Day 12 —

"Conflict is not always the answer."

Proverbs 15:1   ▶︎

A soft answer turns away wrath, but a harsh word stirs up anger.

A fist sometimes feels good.

We want to take action, and we want our frustration resolved now.

At any cost.

Yet the way of the Lord is the gentle word, the softly spoken correction, and the Word of peace. It's the whisper in the time of conflict that will make a difference in how we operate in our efforts to get ahead.

When we speak with the Lord's authority, we draw others unto us. When we lash out with man's authority, people are offended, and they become angry.

"A soft answer turns away wrath." It's not always the easiest way, but it's certainly the best way. Remember this with your family, your co-workers and with people you've just met.

— Day 13 —

"Adapt. It is something that must be done constantly to be able to succeed in the world."

◀❙   *2 Timothy 3:16*   ❙▶

All Scripture is breathed out by God and profitable for teaching, for reproof, for correction, and for training in righteousness.

Many professions require us to update our credentials on a regular basis.

Old procedures become outdated. Systems become more complex. Techniques for success that worked a year ago simply don't cut it any longer.

Even the words we use—jargon—take on new forms, and without adaptation, we're the fossils that can no longer succeed.

In matters of faith, it's also adapt or fail. Our source for our updates is the Bible. The truth in the Word of God never changes, and its application to our lives can be trusted.

Let's get our training cap on. Let's break out the Word, join a Bible study, and get our salvation diploma stamped with our updated credentials. It's how we get our training in righteousness and learn to succeed in the world.

— Day 14 —

"Always seek to push yourself to new heights."

◀   *Matthew 16:19*   ▶

[Jesus said], I will give you the keys of the kingdom of heaven, and whatever you bind on earth shall be bound in heaven, and whatever you loose on earth shall be loosed in heaven.

What's our comfort zone?

Where are the boundaries that make us feel safe?

Jesus tells us we have the keys to do everything He did. There were no limitations on the power of Christ, and we have none on us.

Yet so often we sigh in resignation and wish we could do more for Christ, for our family, and for our community.

We'll find our success when we break out of that soft place where we feel protected and safe. We must push past what we think we're capable of into those things that are hard for us. That's when God stands behind us and keeps us from falling. Christ becomes the source of our power when we're willing to take a chance on Him.

— Day 15 —

"The knowledge that you learn from
making the wrong decision can often be
just as valuable as the knowledge you
learn from making the right decision."

◀│   *James 1:5-8*   │▶

If any of you lacks wisdom, let him ask God, who gives generously
to all without reproach, and it will be given him. But let him ask
in faith, with no doubting, for the one who doubts is like a wave of
the sea that is driven and tossed by the wind. For that person must
not suppose that he will receive anything from the Lord; he is a
double-minded man, unstable in all his ways.

Choice. We choose the red lipstick or the pink. The yellow
tie or the blue. The sweetened tea, or the unsweet.

Many choices don't matter, yet we dare not mess up on the
ones that do. Choose the spouse for money or personality? Pick
the car for practicality or thrills? Walk away from God or walk
toward Him?

Business skills are the same. We make choices. Some are easy
to back out of, and others will bankrupt us.

The knowledge we learn from what goes wrong can be as
valuable as what we learn when it all goes just right.

— Day 16 —

*"To dwell on your regrets is to be lodged
in the past."*

◀   *Philippians 3:13-15*   ▶

*Brothers, I do not consider that I have made it my own. But one
thing I do: forgetting what lies behind and straining forward to
what lies ahead, I press on toward the goal for the prize of the
upward call of God in Christ Jesus. Let those of us who are mature
think this way, and if in anything you think otherwise, God will
reveal that also to you.*

Life is like a long hallway. Each morning, the door to yesterday closes behind us, and we can never open it up or walk
through it again.

We can remember what's behind that door, but it's inaccessible. Worrying about it won't allow us access to it. If we worry
it like a dog with a bone, we'll never move forward in life, and
we'll never find the success God intends for us to have.

Paul says we must forget what lies behind and strain forward
to what lies ahead. In other words, it's the future that holds our
key to success. We won't find it in the past, no matter how much
we chew that old bone.

— Day 17 —

"The path of success is not idle time and waiting. The path to success is hard work and persistence."

◀ *Proverbs 19:15* ▶

Slothfulness casts into a deep sleep, and an idle person will suffer hunger.

There used to be a saying bandied about. *Idle hands are the devil's workshop.*

The meaning's clear. If we're not being industrious in something beneficial, we'll let boredom lead us down the darker road of destruction.

Are we waiting for God's promises to come to us? That's not how God works. If success is our goal, we have two things to do before we will find our success.

1. Work hard, right now, this minute.
2. Keep at it persistently, and never, never give up.

We may feel like we're marking time, and that God's forgotten us, but the truth is much simpler. We're in training. When God perfects us with skills and understanding, then we'll move into His promises and find our success in Him.

— Day 18 —

"Take a step back, look at your life, decide what could be improved, and work every day toward achieving your goal."

◄   *Ephesians 5:1*   ►

Therefore be imitators of God, as beloved children.

What's our standard?

By that we mean, what's the moral backbone on which we base our actions?

Do they match the example of Christ?

Our model for our standard of improvement is found in the Word of God. When we compare our intents, our desires, and our actions to those of the Savior, we'll always find room for improvement.

We can speak kinder, offer more, go further.

There are others who look up to us, and our goal should be to set an example they can respect, in our private lives as well as in public.

The true test of someone's character is how they behave when no one's looking. Let's be as Christ wants us to be.

— Day 19 —

"Once you let your desire for greater success turn into greed, you are stunting your ability to reach your full potential."

◀   1 *Timothy* 6:10   ▶

For the love of money is a root of all kinds of evils. It is through this craving that some have wandered away from the faith and pierced themselves with many pangs.

Do we worry more about our bank account or our giving account?

Wealth is not a problem for God. Rich people can find salvation just as poor people can.

The opposite is true, also. The rich can be distracted by their money, just like the poor.

Read the verse like it's written. For the *love* of money is a root of all kinds of evils. Not *having* money, but *loving* it.

When our desire for money consumes us, we lose sight of God and the good He wishes us to do. Kindness to others, generosity, and material support of the local church fall to the wayside. Christ must be our focus, so that God can bring out our full potential in Him.

— Day 20 —

"Watch closely, for if you can learn from the mistakes of others, then you can prevent yourself from making the same errors."

◀︎   1 John 1:9   ▶︎

If we confess our sins, he is faithful and just to forgive us our sins and to cleanse us from all unrighteousness.

History repeats itself.

What goes around comes around.

Be careful when you live in a glass house.

All these are true, but they don't have to be. The truth is, each generation comes to the table anew, and we find the same old ways to stumble in our pursuit of survival.

History repeats itself when we don't change our wrongdoing. What comes back to us is our reward for what we've done. Our glass house is fragile, and it can tumble down unexpectedly.

We can't change on our own. Only through Christ can we find the strength to avoid the errors of the previous generation. Only through confession of our sins can we find salvation in Him.

— Day 21 —

"Whether it be today or in 20 years, you will always face the consequences of your actions."

◁   Galatians 6:7   ▷

Do not be deceived: God is not mocked, for whatever one sows, that will he also reap.

The Internet is forever.

If we've posted, tweeted, or commented on something, someone has it saved somewhere. If we delete our words or our images, it's too late. They are stored on someone's hard drive to haunt us one day.

Even our idle online searches are stored, never to be erased.

Harsh words are the same way. Remembered comments, actions, or intents will erupt when we least expect them.

We don't "get away" with things we think we've hidden. They just haven't come to light. When the secret places are revealed, what truths do we want to be exposed?

Let's sow kindness, goodness, and generosity. Our legacy must be one of Christian brotherhood, offered unto the world.

— Day 22 —

"Do not let a failure shake your
foundation."

◀   Matthew 7:24   ▶

"Everyone then who hears these words of mine and does them will
be like a wise man who built his house on the rock."

Rock is one of the strongest building materials we have.

Wood will rot away within a generation. Plaster, asphalt, and cement are poor substitutes.

When we want a building to stand forever, we dig to bedrock to set our foundation. Then storms or floods cannot bring it down.

Our moral fiber is our stone underpinning. We build our foundation from the Word of God. Then when failures dog our path, we will have the rock that is Christ for our firm footing. Our foundation will be in Him, for we've placed our trust in our Lord.

Wisdom breeds success, and our wisest move is to base our moral fiber on the teachings of Christ. We'll find our fortitude in Him, and we'll move closer to success every day.

— Day 23 —

*"Do you just want to be happy or to
actually make a difference in this world?"*

◀| *James 2:26* |▶

*For as the body apart from the spirit is dead, so also faith apart
from works is dead.*

What gives us happiness?

It must be indulgence. To do what we want. Gluttony,
laziness, and debauchery. The call of our senses, right?

All that is physical, and yes, much of it is temporarily pleas-
ing to the body. However, it can't satisfy the inside part of who
we are.

Helping others. That's one way to be fulfilled. Volunteering.
Sacrificing to make someone else happy. Giving of ourselves even
when we think others don't care. And most importantly, serving
Christ.

Intentions without actions are spurious and ineffective. We
must do something, we must *act*, to make a difference in the lives
of others. Success-Speak offers us a fresh direction; it's our actions
that tell the level of our faith in Christ.

— Day 24 —

"To truly be successful in the fullest sense of the word, you must succeed in all aspects of life . . . not just one."

◀   John 14:6   ▶

Jesus said to him, "I am the way, and the truth, and the life. No one comes to the Father except through me."

Financial success is like holding one arm of a starfish. Without the rest, the creature is incomplete.

The animal can't live a full life. Its potential will never be realized.

Our goals for success must include our family life, our leisure time, and our work relationships. There's no area that can be left out. Our spirituality can't be excluded from the mix, either. Our relationship with the Father, through the blood of Christ shed on the cross, affects every part of who we are.

The starfish is a whole creature only when all its arms are present and accounted for.

We become spiritually whole through salvation in Christ, and we achieve true, fulfilling success in the world when we include the people who share our days.

— Day 25 —

*"Who will you be? You can either be the
one watching the world change around
you, or you can be the one changing the
world. It's time to make a choice."*

◀︎   *Joshua 1:9*   ▶︎

*Have I not commanded you? Be strong and courageous. Do not be
frightened, and do not be dismayed, for the LORD your God is with
you wherever you go.*

Old LP records were designed to be played one side at a time.

They had songs on both sides, but you could only listen to one side or the other. When you started up the music, you had to decide which side to play. A choice had to be made.

If you didn't like the song that was playing, you could turn the record over and listen to the other side.

We can choose to be courageous and change the world. It's a decision. A choice. If we don't like the way our life is going, it's not the only song we have to play.

Flip the record over. Make a choice for success. Get out there and change the world.

God is with you wherever you go.

— Day 26 —

"Even the person who walks straight and true for his entire life will have made mistakes, fallen, and inadvertently damaged the lives of others. Apologize and move on."

◀ᴵ　　　1 Peter 1:22　　　ᴵ▶

Having purified your souls by your obedience to the truth for a sincere brotherly love, love one another earnestly from a pure heart.

We can't avoid offending some people.

They are looking for barbs to catch on their sour attitudes, and we can't keep out of their way.

No matter how hard we try.

Our only option is to make sure our lives are lived to a holy standard, to be kind in our words, speak softly when we must confront someone, and have a thick skin when others lash out at us.

Then we apologize for any offense we've caused, and we let it go. We are travelers in this life. Yesterday is another country, and all the borders are closed. We can't relive the day that's already done. We leave with Jesus the hurts others can't release, and we move forward into tomorrow's success with a clear conscience and a pure heart.

— Day 27 —

"A single word or action can bring down the mightiest and devastate someone emotionally and physically. Choose your words and actions with care."

◀   Psalm 19:14   ▶

Let the words of my mouth and the meditation of my heart be acceptable in your sight, O LORD, my rock and my redeemer.

The tongue is mightier than the sword.

That's not Edward Bulwer-Lytton's original quote from 1839, but it certainly fits today's quick-moving and pervasive social media situation.

What we say can do more damage than an entire army of well-outfitted soldiers. One tweet. One post. One inappropriate image. We can damage people emotionally, undermine business dealings, or divide loyalties to bring countries to the brink of war.

Our gauge for what's acceptable must be the Word of God. Christ is our rock and our redeemer. In our thoughts, in our quiet time, and with our voice in front of others, we must be pure in what we say and do.

It's the soft word that counts when we want to be kind to those around us.

— Day 28 —

"Do you like what you see around yourself? Do you want things to be different? Then change them. Yes, bringing about change is that simple."

◀   *Romans 12:2*   ▶

Do not be conformed to this world, but be transformed by the renewal of your mind, that by testing you may discern what is the will of God, what is good and acceptable and perfect.

We join country clubs in our social circles, denominations in our churches, and cliques in our schools.

We have a need to group with people of a like kind, even if we must exclude others in the process.

Have we thrown in our lot with Christ, or is the world our choice of clubs?

If we don't like the situation around us; if there's something we want to be different; if we don't like who we are or the situation we're in, we don't have to live with it.

Our method of change comes from God. We renew our minds by thinking on Him, studying the Word, and spending time with people who also desire to be like Christ. In Him, we become better than we were before.

— Day 29 —

*"You must be the one to make the choice
to become successful."*

◀   John 15:16   ▶

*[Jesus said], You did not choose me, but I chose you and appointed
you that you should go and bear fruit and that your fruit should
abide, so that whatever you ask the Father in my name, he may
give it to you.*

To go or stay, to bear fruit or be barren, to ask in the Father's
name or do without.

It's all a choice, and it's in our hands.

What do we want out of life? Salvation is waiting on us. Jesus
tells us He's already chosen us. All we need to do is respond.

Our success in the other areas of our life is already out there
for us. We can go or stay, achieve our goals or not, step out in
faith or do without.

No one should look at his or her circumstance and see an
impenetrable wall. There is no hedge too high to climb over.
Some may have it easier than others, but we can all find success.
It's waiting on us to move forward.

— Day 30 —

*"Success requires persistence during the
worst of times."*

◀| *Galatians 6:9* |▶

*And let us not grow weary of doing good, for in due season we will
reap, if we do not give up.*

A ship sails best in calm seas. The cargo remains undamaged,
and the passengers enjoy the ride. The crew are calm and relaxed,
with time to make sure their guests are comfortable and safe.

Everyone wants to be aboard when the sun shines bright.

What about when the storm blows in? The ship rocks from
side to side. Furniture moves from its established location. Eating
is next to impossible, and there's nothing to do except hang on.
The ship will still make it to port, but it will require extraordinary
effort. Everyone will have to work harder.

Success in our personal lives plays out in a similar fashion.
There'll be days when our ship rocks side to side, and we're barely
hanging on. We must trust in our Lord, for He is our safety net,
our captain, and our helpful crew. He is the one that provides for
His children, so that we can make it through.

— Day 31 —

"If you are lodged in the past, the future will slip past you, and along with it, your chances for success."

◀   Proverbs 16:9   ▶

The heart of man plans his way, but the LORD establishes his steps.

Walking backwards is never a good idea.

The only way to see where we're going is to face forward. Remember the story of Lot's wife. As they were escaping the destruction of Sodom, she turned to see what she'd left behind, only to become a pillar of salt.

What's back there is in the past. The doors are closed, the way is blocked, and we can't return, no matter how hard we try.

Imagine a butterfly being chased by a bird and trying to get back inside its cocoon. It can't do it. It might seem like a place of safety, but that opportunity has come and gone.

We can only move forward.

We plan, and the Lord establishes our steps. We can imagine what we want out of life, but our only assurance comes when we turn things over to God and forge ahead into our future.

— Day 32 —

"Have you told Jesus 'thank you' today? If not, you should do so right now."

◀ *1 Thessalonians 5:18* ▶

Give thanks in all circumstances; for this is the will of God in Christ Jesus for you.

Gratitude improves our attitude.

Think about it. When we wake up in a bad mood, it seems that everything goes wrong all day. On a good day, nothing can spoil our joy.

We've heard of Norman Vincent Peale's *The Power of Positive Thinking*. Essentially, it tells us that we can change our life by our outlook on the world. When we say bright and positive things, we'll find our attitude begins to reflect our words, and we'll have better days because of it.

What's God done for you today? Write it down. Remember it. Tell God thanks. It can be for a sunny morning, or even our breakfast. Anything. We'll find that the more we pay attention, the longer our list will grow.

Remember, gratitude improves our life. Give it a try.

— Day 33 —

"Learn about the world around you.
Observe it, study its history, and
understand the mistakes it has made.
Only then can you truly make progress."

◀ *Romans 15:4* ▶

For whatever was written in former days was written for our
instruction, that through endurance and through the
encouragement of the Scriptures we might have hope.

Battleships are impressive pieces of machinery.

Yet their usefulness is limited in modern warfare. They've been superseded by long-range cruise missiles, modern aircraft, and remotely flown drones.

We can learn from our historical use of battleships, but we don't want to depend solely on them in the 21st century. To do so would be a dire mistake.

We should take the past and learn from it, but we don't live in it. History should be our springboard to progress ahead of where we've been.

Through endurance and encouragement, we can find hope for a brighter future, for ourselves and those around us. We find our hope in the scriptures, for our future in is God.

— Day 34 —

"Even if you seek perfection, to cause no harm, or to just do all the good you can achieve, know that the success will still come bound with occasional failures."

◀   Romans 5:3-5   ▶

More than that, we rejoice in our sufferings, knowing that suffering produces endurance, and endurance produces character, and character produces hope, and hope does not put us to shame, because God's love has been poured into our hearts through the Holy Spirit who has been given to us.

There is no perfect life.

We can't live it, be it, or create it. It's the human condition, that things go wrong, we are misunderstood, or our intentions go awry when we least expect.

Failure is part of who we are.

We must distinguish between experiencing a failure and becoming a failure. In other words, do we let the failure become us, or do we turn it on its head and make the failure a stepping stone to our future success?

Failure produces endurance . . . character . . . and hope. We never have to be ashamed when we find our faith in God.

— Day 35 —

*"Your greatest strength comes when you
turn loose of your reservations."*

◀   Deuteronomy 31:6   ▶

*Be strong and courageous. Do not fear or be in dread of them, for it
is the LORD your God who goes with you. He will not leave you or
forsake you.*

A reservation, by definition, is something we're holding
back.

In a restaurant, we hold a table for an arriving guest. Their
reservation is a special place for no one else.

When we reserve our skills or desires, we hold them back.
We don't use them, and we don't allow anyone else to, either.
We hold them in reservation, many times because we dread the
outcome if we're unsuccessful.

God says to be strong and courageous. He will be with us.
We can't be afraid of success. If we want to find it, God will
champion us, and He will be with us all the way.

When we turn loose, our reservations are no longer a noose
to keep us from our upcoming success.

— Day 36 —

"Do not fear living your life to its greatest potential."

◀ *Ephesians 2:10* ▶

For we are his workmanship, created in Christ Jesus for good works, which God prepared beforehand, that we should walk in them.

Modern phones are wonderous machines.

We can call from almost anywhere, and that's a striking achievement.

Yet, if all we do is make phone calls, we've missed out on many things our phones will do. We can text, take pictures, surf the Internet, get directions, even make video calls, all at a touch on the screen. We have a calculator, a GPS device, and a flashlight, all in one.

Yes, a flashlight. Those come on our modern phones.

What are we missing out on in ourselves? God has built all sorts of possibilities into every one of us. We are created for good works, ones that God has already prepared for us, ones we should get involved in. That's our design, and in God, we can live out our potential and find our success in Him.

— Day 37 —

*"There is only one person on this earth
with the power to prevent you from
reaching your full potential and achieving
success beyond your wildest dreams. That
person is you!"*

◀ 1 Corinthians 3:8 ▶

*He who plants and he who waters are one, and each will receive his
wages according to his labor.*

We get what we've got coming to us.

We often see that as a negative thing, but it's not. You see, we really do get what's coming to us. According to this verse, we plant our crops, we water them, and we get paid for the work we've done.

The harder we work, the better our paycheck.

When we truly desire to achieve success, we'll set other things aside to achieve it. We'll leave the television off, skip parties, and work late into the night to get where we want to go.

There's nothing too arduous when we have our dreams driving us on.

We can never slow down. Frustration may batter us, but our labor will be rewarded. Never give up, and we'll find success.

— Day 38 —

"Don't let your chance for success slip away just because the path becomes rocky."

Philippians 4:6   ▶

Do not be anxious about anything, but in everything by prayer and supplication with thanksgiving let your requests be made known to God.

Every mountain starts in the foothills. We begin on a shallow path. It's only when we near the peak that we must don our gloves and steady ourselves as we climb.

It's preparation that keeps us safe on the rocky sections. It's the long walk up the grassy slopes that develops our muscles, helps us build our stamina, and gives us the skills that make our journey a success.

We can't let a few rough patches dissuade us from moving forward. A slope of rocky scree isn't the entire journey. Our faith in our goal is what gives us the determination to keep heading upward.

We climb our spiritual mountains best while on our knees. With Success-Speak for our starting point, we can climb our mountain with faith in the goal we want to achieve.

— Day 39 —

"If you don't know what to do, then it may be time for you to find yourself a role model."

◀   *1 Timothy 4:12*   ▶

Let no one despise you for your youth, but set the believers an example in speech, in conduct, in love, in faith, in purity.

Role models come in all sizes and shapes.

There's no age requirement, gender entitlement, or admonition that a role model must be financially wealthy.

Instead, find people who are good at what you want to do. Search out those who've become successful in your desired field. Strike up friendships. Hang out with them.

Learn from them.

Your role model may come in the form of a friend, a parent, an uncle or aunt, or a grandparent. Perhaps it's someone at work, even your boss. You can find them at the gym, shopping in the grocery store, or standing behind the pulpit on Sunday morning.

What do you look for in your role model? Clean speech, admirable conduct, and high standards in love, faith, and purity.

— Day 40 —

"You can overcome any obstacle."

◀   *2 Timothy 1:7*   ▶

For God gave us a spirit not of fear but of power and love and self-control.

A fallen tree on a forest service road can defeat the most intrepid backwoodsman.

If we're unprepared, we're not getting past, four-wheel-drive or not. We must be prepared before we set out, so that success can be ours.

Our chainsaw is the power of Christ, and with it, we can slice the obstacles away, clearing our forward path.

Our hiking boots are our Christian love, for with it, we can navigate the muddy detours and relocate the trail.

Our toolbelt is our God-given self-control, for it enables us to be empowered in any situation.

When we are attuned to the Spirit of God, we'll find success in every situation.

— Day 41 —

"You must surmount the obstructions in your path if you truly desire to succeed."

◀ Galatians 5:13 ▶

For you were called to freedom, brothers. Only do not use your freedom as an opportunity for the flesh, but through love serve one another.

What ball-and-chain do we wear?

Is it our lack of education? An abusive past? Or does economics keep us from moving forward in life?

Whatever it is, we must toss it aside.

Whatever it takes to unlock the chain, to wriggle free, to get ourselves out of that situation, that's what we must do.

Then comes the tough part.

We can't let ourselves get trapped again, not by desires for things of the flesh, or by searching for things that satisfy our physical desires.

Instead, we must ask how we can help others to find success in their lives. We'll move forward together.

— Day 42 —

"It's not the obstacles in your life that determine who you are; it's your decisions."

◀ *James 1:12* ▮▶

Blessed is the man who remains steadfast under trial, for when he has stood the test he will receive the crown of life, which God has promised to those who love him.

Imagine a man driving to work. He gets halfway there to discover a repair crew blocking the street.

That's it. He may as well go home.

Wrong! If he turns around and returns home, he's made the decision not to be successful.

It's called thinking laterally. If the direct route won't get us where we want to go, what alternatives do we have?

All sorts of things will block our way through life: financial pressures, interpersonal conflicts, or health concerns. If we want to find success, our decision must be to succeed.

Even when we come to a dead end, our decision to move past our obstacle is the choice that will lead us to success.

— Day 43 —

"Act on every good opportunity. Make your move now."

◀   *Psalm 62:12*   ▶

And that to you, O Lord, belongs steadfast love. For you will render to a man according to his work.

Just get out there and do it!

We hear this from coaches, shoe companies, and motivational experts. They are all correct, too.

We need to quit overthinking and get into the action zone. No one ever got rewarded for sitting at home and saying, "I thought of that first."

We must get into motion and start doing *something* if we want to find our success in life.

That job opportunity you didn't take? Someone's working today. That house you didn't buy? Someone's living there. That car you let pass you by? It's being driven by someone. The investment that frightened you off?

You're getting it. It's time to make your move.

— Day 44 —

*"Do not let yourself be defeated by
something as simple as a lack of faith."*

◄I   *Matthew 21:22*   I►

And whatever you ask in prayer, you will receive, if you have faith.

Faith is something we use every day.

We flip on the light switch, and we know the light will come on. We don't do anything to power the bulb. That happens miles away. We have no control over it, either.

We know it's faith, because it surprises us if it doesn't happen. We blink, flip the switch a few times, and must check yet another switch before we admit that the electricity is out.

Then we head to the breaker box to get it started again.

That's how we should be in what we ask out of life. We should simply expect it to happen. If it doesn't, we should flip the switch a few times, then move on to try another one.

We don't expect that the electric company has quit making power, because they haven't. We just need to find the breaker, flip it, and try once again. That's how we find success in life.

— Day 45 —

"You need to be cautious to not lose your moral base, the foundation that is who you are."

◀   1 Thessalonians 5:21   ▶

But test everything; hold fast what is good.

Quality control is vital.

If a company manufactures seals for automotive engines, and they continually fail, soon that company will face a backlash, and their sales will go down the drain.

It doesn't matter if 90% are of excellent quality. That 10% will ruin their reputation.

As Christians, we face the same dilemma. If we follow the precepts of Christ nine times out of ten, it's that tenth time that will ruin our Christian witness.

People will remember that one time we let our principles slip, and they won't trust what we have to say.

The same applies in the world of business. When we stay on track by using sound principles, treating others fairly, and respecting the values of Christ, we're poised for success in Him.

— Day 46 —

"Balance your desire for advancement with wisdom. An overstep can cost you everything."

◀| Matthew 6:33 |▶

But seek first the kingdom of God and his righteousness, and all these things will be added to you.

Distraction is a primary reason we don't find success.

An opportunity to make a buck gets in the way of going to college, and we drop out.

We decide to buy the fancy truck rather than invest in our 401K.

We choose what feels good rather than what we know is right. Self-fulfillment. Me first. Let me have what I want now.

Move too far the wrong direction, and we step onto unstable ground. We must ask ourselves where we're headed, and if our current actions will help us get there.

Seek ye first the kingdom of God . . . is the best choice we can make. The Father will be there to guide us, and we'll have the hand of the Master over everything we do.

— Day 47 —

"Some things can only truly be understood through experiencing them yourself."

◀   *Job 12:12*   ▶

Wisdom is with the aged, and understanding in length of days.

In some cultures, old people are revered.

We give them respect, because of their long lives and the lessons they can impart.

It's experience that gives us an emotional connection to events. What's outside our direct realm of experience is distant and meaningless to us.

People who lived through the terrorist attacks of the World Trade Center or the Boston Marathon bombing feel *impelled* to counter terrorism.

The way we interact with others follows the same principle. When we've been wronged or abused, we feel empathy for others in the same situation.

Let's get out there and experience life. Then share that with others, so that they can have the benefit of what we know.

— Day 48 —

*"Move on, overcome, and know that your
past is not the future."*

◄| *John 16:33* |►

*I have said these things to you, that in me you may have peace. In
the world you will have tribulation. But take heart; I have
overcome the world.*

People struggle with all sorts of issues.

Haters. Shamers. Emotional abusers.

Some are even assaulted, simply because they are an easy target, either in their appearance or their beliefs.

Our past is not an indicator of what we can achieve. We must find a way to put the events of yesterday into a box that we never open, so that we can live in today.

We will need to do this over and over. Life isn't going to leave us alone to "get on with things." Some of us will be hated, shamed, and even assaulted. It happens. Move on. Overcome. Be stronger than we think we can be.

Christ will be our strength to help us overcome the world.

— Day 49 —

*"It isn't until you have lost everything,
that you truly know what you had."*

◀   *Isaiah 41:10*   ▶

*Fear not, for I am with you; be not dismayed, for I am your God; I
will strengthen you, I will help you, I will uphold you with my
righteous right hand.*

The status quo is easy to fall back on.

What we live is what we're used to. We accept our daily lives
as the norm and expect that others live about the same.

Do we have a good car? We forget that others don't.

What about food? Do we think of the hungry?

Air conditioning and the Internet. There are those that do
without.

It's in times of distress, when the car strands us, when we
can't get to the store, or when the electricity goes out that we're
reminded of the goodness of God.

Our God is our strength through our trials. When we
remember others and offer aid, God is pleased with us.

— Day 50 —

"Don't ever stand still. You must be
moving forward and reaching for your
goals."

◀ᴵ   *1 Corinthians 9:24*   ᴵ▶

Do you not know that in a race all the runners run, but only one
receives the prize? So run that you may obtain it.

In the Parable of the Talents, three men are given monetary investments to watch over while their master goes on a long trip.

Two get a good return on their money, and they are rewarded.

The third hides his in the ground, returning to his master exactly what he was given.

It didn't turn out well for him. His money was taken from him and given to the others.

What are our skills? We must use them, put them into practice. Can we write a good, well-constructed sentence? Find a way to use that skill in the local church. Is shopping our forte? We can volunteer to pick up food for the elderly. Then when our opportunity comes along, we'll be primed to move forward into our success.

— Day 51 —

"Always walk forward, never backward."

◀   *Luke 9:56*   ▶

And they went on to another village.

This verse falls at the end of a passage about a Samaritan village that rejected Jesus. It reveals something vital about our Lord.

Even Jesus accepted there were times when it was better to simply move on. He knew that untenable situations can't always be resolved. If we become mired in our present circumstance, we become useless to others, a rock that will become a stumbling block.

What's our Samaritan village? What keeps us from our success?

If our Lord had become stuck in that village, trying to work things out, He never would have made it to Jerusalem, where many of our Biblical truths were recorded.

Success comes in the next steps we take, not the ones we should be leaving behind.

— Day 52 —

"Seeing and believing are two very different things."

◂   *John 20:29*   ▸

Jesus said to him, "Have you believed because you have seen me? Blessed are those who have not seen and yet have believed."

We are a reach-out-and-touch-it society.

What we can't hold in our hands has no substance to us.

The most successful people can put aside today's desires to achieve their plans for tomorrow.

This is a vital lesson in our relationship with Christ. We can't see Him in the flesh in the present moment. We must have faith that He's there, and that one day He'll return for us.

If we believe in something, we can step into its truth, and it will change who we are.

If you can't see your success today, don't let that stop you from believing you'll find it tomorrow. If you can't *see* it, yet you still have the faith to *believe* it, your success will be yours.

Don't let the world confuse you. Your success is up to you.

— Day 53 —

"Not all battles are worth fighting."

◀   *Colossians 2:8*   ▶

See to it that no one takes you captive by philosophy and empty deceit, according to human tradition, according to the elemental spirits of the world, and not according to Christ.

Some people like argument for argument's sake.

Others are incensed when everyone doesn't agree with them.

We must decide whether a battle carries us toward our goal or distracts us from it. If a battle knocks us off our feet, we must dust ourselves off and get back on the field. If a battle sidelines us, skewing us from our goal, we need to run to God and let Him get us back on track.

We must be single-minded. That means we can only focus on one thing: the goal we desire to achieve. Anything else is a distraction we can't afford.

If our battle doesn't benefit us, it's worthless for achieving our goal. Let's focus on Christ. Let's face ahead. Let's move forward into success.

— Day 54 —

*"Let your past experiences strengthen you
for the future."*

Ephesians 6:10   ▶

Finally, be strong in the Lord and in the strength of his might.

Recovery after a disaster is difficult.

In 2017, Puerto Rico was hit by a devastating hurricane. The power grid was wiped out across the entire island.

People posted, "We need water! We're dying!"

Months later, they still struggled with their appalling situation. Some authorities said it would be years before the island recovered.

The people had to find strength to be able to face their future.

We all face disasters, spiritual, financial, or like Puerto Rico, ones of life or death. We can't always resolve them easily.

Our option is to find strength to make it through. We find our spiritual strength in the Lord, for in Him, we can do what we can't accomplish on our own.

— Day 55 —

"Every failed attempt is an opportunity to learn."

◀   Revelation 14:12   ▶

Here is a call for the endurance of the saints, those who keep the commandments of God and their faith in Jesus.

If at first you don't succeed . . .

We know the rest. *We must try, try again.*

The bigger picture is that we learn a little more each time we make a repeated attempt. We become smarter.

It doesn't mean we enjoy failing. We take the time to see it as an opportunity. We look for the improvements we can make, and we incorporate them into our future actions.

Spiritually, we may slip up. We can't achieve the perfection of Christ, not while we are on this earth. We are imitators of Him, only, but that can't distract us from modeling our actions after His.

In the business world, in our family, and in our personal life, that also holds true. Never quit reaching toward your goal.

— Day 56 —

"The direction taken is often more dependent upon someone's views rather than the actual facts."

◀   *Psalm 32:8*   ▶

I will instruct you and teach you in the way you should go; I will counsel you with my eye upon you.

Facts can lie.

They tell us that we can't be more than we are. We don't have enough experience or the right education. We *can't* be successful because we *aren't* successful.

It's our determination that tells the truth of things.

We will succeed. We're determined. Nothing will get in our way.

The Lord says He will instruct and teach us. That means we can depend on Him for direction. He will be at our side. He will aide us.

He will guide us when we don't know what to do or where to go.

It's our destination that determines who we are.

— Day 57 —

"Impatience results in mistakes just as accidents cause death."

◀   *James 5:7-8*   ▶

Be patient, therefore, brothers, until the coming of the Lord. See how the farmer waits for the precious fruit of the earth, being patient about it, until it receives the early and the late rains. You also, be patient. Establish your hearts, for the coming of the Lord is at hand.

Have you ever made pancakes, the sort you mix in a bowl and pour into a skillet?

Once you pour the batter, it's important to let it sit until the batter begins to firm up. Then you can turn it to brown the other side.

Flip it too early, and the batter will still be liquid and will go everywhere.

It's called patience, no matter how hungry you are.

Finding success is the same. You must take time to attend the classes. Work the night shift. Get the experience. Success comes through hard work and believing in yourself.

— Day 58 —

"Is the cost worth the gain? That is a question you must ask yourself for everything you want."

◂ Proverbs 22:7 ▸

The rich rules over the poor, and the borrower is the slave of the lender.

Success is desirable for a reason.

Those at the top of the food chain have authority over those further down.

We must consider every decision. What we decide now affects us later on, often for the rest of our lives.

If we take on student debt, how will that affect our job prospects? Will we be happy in a high-paying field we dislike? Can we make enough in our preferred profession to travel like we envision?

The reality is that we must live within our means, and that forces us to make hard choices. The city house, or move to the suburbs? New car or used? One kid or two?

Everything has a cost. It's up to us to decide.

— Day 59 —

"How well you have succeeded is determined not only by what has been achieved, but how you handled the failures."

◀ *Romans 8:1* ▶

There is therefore now no condemnation for those who are in Christ Jesus.

Buy a good pair of hiking boots and head up the side of a mountain.

On the way, you might have to retreat a time or two to find a better path.

When you reach the top, do you celebrate the victory or moan over how many times you had to retrace your steps? No one will criticize you for the times you backed up along the way. The only thing that matters is whether you achieved your goal.

Try that attitude in life. Set your life goal ten, twenty, or thirty years away. Quit seeing the small misdirection that happened yesterday or today as your life in ruins. Get a calendar. Mark your successes. Go back and reread them. Cheer yourself on with coffee and cake. You'll feel better for it.

When you pick yourself up, you've succeeded in moving on.

— Day 60 —

"Don't fear what you don't know. It's the unknown that brings forth greatness, achievement, and more importantly, success."

◀   Psalm 34:4   ▶

I sought the LORD, and he answered me and delivered me from all my fears.

Graveyards reveal the truth of the human condition.

Look at the years on each tombstone. An entire life is revealed in the dash that comes between birth and death.

We start out on one side of the equation, we blink a few times, and our dash is complete. Our life is done.

When we begin, it's all an unknown. Each day, each month, each year. We have no idea how it will work out. We can plan, but the Lord guides our footsteps.

Why be afraid? Life is a banquet, there for our feasting and enjoyment. Each day is a bite of goodness that we must savor before it's gone.

One day, our dash will tell the story of our life. Make sure to live it, without fear, in Christ, and achieving every goal.

— Day 61 —

"Once your doubts are overcome, there will be no stopping you."

◀   Matthew 21:21   ▶

And Jesus answered them, "Truly, I say to you, if you have faith and do not doubt, you will not only do what has been done to the fig tree, but even if you say to this mountain, 'Be taken up and thrown into the sea,' it will happen."

How hard would it be to tightrope walk over Niagara Falls?

Impossible, you say? Nik Wallenda did it in 2012, and he had no problem at all.

The next year, he tightrope walked the Grand Canyon, then moved on to Chicago to repeat his feat, this time between city buildings.

Where are our doubts causing us to fail? Where do we lack faith? Our first step to overcoming our doubts is to learn to trust in the little things. Can we hold down a job? Is our paycheck enough? Does God really answer prayer?

Once we get past that, the mountain will be thrown into the sea, and nothing will be outside our grasp.

— Day 62 —

"If you stray from the path of what is right, don't surrender; you must stand up and step back onto the path of that which is worthwhile and righteous."

◀   *James 4:7*   ▶

Submit yourselves therefore to God. Resist the devil, and he will flee from you.

Giving in to a bully is never a good idea.

When you let the bully see that he has power over you, it simply makes him stronger.

He'll come against you harder next time.

Our only option is to make our stand. We can never back down. That's true in our spiritual life, our business dealings, and in our personal relationships.

God is our spiritual stronghold. When we let Him be our strong tower, we no longer have to worry about our future.

When the world seems to knock us down, we must stand up, square our shoulders, and raise our head. The fight is on.

Never take the easy road. Always find the way that's right, and let it be your guide your entire life.

— Day 63 —

"If you do not have the mental attitude of success and the faith to persevere, your potential will go unfulfilled."

◀ *2 Thessalonians 3:13* ▶

As for you, brothers, do not grow weary in doing good.

It's reaching the finish line that counts.

The New York Marathon is a 6.5-hour, 26-mile race that will tax the most astute athlete. Yet, more than 50,000 people show up annually to attempt the course.

Why? To complete the race, of course. For many, it's not whether they win, but simply the knowledge that they've run the entire distance. It takes all their will, and to give up before the end is as devastating a defeat as they can imagine.

How willing are we to chase after our success? Do we continue even when we're exhausted? Do mockers dismay us? Or is our internal fortitude enough to smash all the roadblocks in our way?

Once we start on the road to success, the finish line is our goal. We can't look to the left or the right, but straight ahead. Defeat can never be allowed to run at our side.

— Day 64 —

"Just because you are victorious doesn't mean you are the winner. Were the sacrifices to achieve the victory worth the cost?"

◀   *Hebrews 13:15*   ▶

Through him then let us continually offer up a sacrifice of praise to God, that is, the fruit of lips that acknowledge his name.

We often see someone's large home and shiny car as a measure of success.

It's our mark of victory in the dog-eat-dog world of modern business. We've achieved the prize, and all the money is ours.

Yet, what about our spouse? Our children? The people we left behind?

If our company is at the top of the financial markets, and we've wiped out a thousand jobs, what about those workers? Have we helped them win?

Or were they sacrifices along the way?

God's approval is our mark of success. We can offer praise unto His name by acknowledging His helping hand in everything we do.

— Day 65 —

"Find somebody you can look up to. Look at their life, how they failed and succeeded. Take that knowledge and use it to create your own success."

◀ *Jeremiah 29:11* ▶

For I know the plans I have for you, declares the LORD, plans for welfare and not for evil, to give you a future and a hope.

Google a list of the titans of industry, the financial shakers and movers of the past 50 years. Focus on the men and women in the field that interests you. Read about them to learn what they did right and where they messed up.

Search out their faults and how they overcame them. Discover how they turned what was bad into something good.

Can we repeat what they did? Not exactly. Circumstances are different for everyone. However, we can set ourselves up for success using the same parameters they used to move up the ladder, and up and up.

When we ask God to be our guide and our dependable source of power, we've taken our first step on the road to success. With Him at the head of what we do, nothing will stand in our way.

— Day 66 —

"Know who you were, know who you are, and most importantly, know who you want to be."

James 4:13-15   ►

Come now, you who say, "Today or tomorrow we will go into such and such a town and spend a year there and trade and make a profit"— yet you do not know what tomorrow will bring. What is your life? For you are a mist that appears for a little time and then vanishes. Instead you ought to say, "If the Lord wills, we will live and do this or that."

The future is a decision that hasn't yet been made. You can take aim in any direction you desire.

Here's the caveat we all face: Tomorrow is out of our control.

Flexibility is the key to making your future work for you. Make plans, determine what you want, then see where God takes you. Success-Speak will focus you in the right direction.

Your success might be immediate, or it might be a long time in coming. It's time to get ready to move ahead.

If the Lord wills . . . is all about preparation. When you're ready, God is prepared to move you into your position of power.

— Day 67 —

*"It's how you handle the challenges you
face that define you."*

◀   *James 1:2-4*   ▶

*Count it all joy, my brothers, when you meet trials of various kinds,
for you know that the testing of your faith produces steadfastness.
And let steadfastness have its full effect, that you may be perfect and
complete, lacking in nothing.*

Look at a boxer's face when he's accepting his winning belt.

It might be scarred and bloody, and an eye or two might be swollen, but there'll be a grin on his face.

He's won the contest!

Yet there's a good chance he went down a time or two. He's taken a licking and had to endure pain. He's faced his challenges, gotten back up, and continued to fight.

That's what counts when you've overcome your challenges. You've won! You've defeated your enemy!

All of life is like that. We get knocked down, lick our wounds, get back up, and conquer the challenge. Let's do it!

— Day 68 —

"It isn't whether something's actually possible, as all things are possible. It's whether you believe it's possible."

◀ John 14:12-14 ▶

Truly, truly, I say to you, whoever believes in me will also do the works that I do; and greater works than these will he do, because I am going to the Father. Whatever you ask in my name, this I will do, that the Father may be glorified in the Son. If you ask me anything in my name, I will do it.

Successful people continually give the same piece of advice:

Set your goals just outside your comfort zone, not so far that you can't reach them, but just far enough that you must stretch a bit.

Then you must believe. Totally. One hundred percent.

Jesus said it this way: *Whoever believes in me . . . whatever you ask in my name . . . I will do it.*

That's a conditional promise, where we must do something first. Believe, then receive.

It works in every part of our lives. Faith works miracles.

— Day 69 —

"Don't let yourself get too deeply embedded in events. It is wise to stop, take a step back, and see the complete picture."

◀   *James 4:10*   ▶

Humble yourselves before the Lord, and he will exalt you.

How can we determine if we're on the path to our goals?

There's a saying that we can't see the forest for the trees, which has an element of truth. We also can't see our collapsing family because of our anger toward our spouse. We can't tell the business is crumbling, because we're keeping up appearances. We can't tell our success tactics aren't working, because we've already started to brag to our friends.

We need off the mechanical bull. It's time to get our feet onto solid ground, so that we can revaluate where we are and where we need to go.

It's known as humility. Not getting too proud. Once we see who we really are, our goals will come into focus, and we'll have no trouble making our way to where we need to be.

God exalts those whom He will. He chooses the humble of heart to stand tall for Him.

— Day 70 —

"The first step to improving your life is setting the goal of who you want to be."

4I   Proverbs 21:5   I▶

The plans of the diligent lead surely to abundance, but everyone who is hasty comes only to poverty.

Impulse control—or the lack of it—is what drives much of the U.S. economy.

We want to be like the Joneses, with a bigger house, nicer watches, and vacations on par to none.

We'll do better to plan according to what we have available; decide how we're going to move ahead; set a goal and determine the steps necessary to achieve it.

We can't do only what feels good today. That's a disaster, offering no more than a temporary surge of good feelings.

Our better bet is to pace ourselves, so that our goal can be ours. Keep a little money in the bank. Take shorter vacations. Work a few hours of overtime.

When we keep our focus on our goal, our future is assured.

— Day 71 —

"Don't expect rational actions from irrational people."

◀   *Matthew 5:17*   ▶

Do not think that I have come to abolish the Law or the Prophets; I have not come to abolish them but to fulfill them.

These are the words of the Master.

Christ is our example to live our lives in a way that follows the rules and makes sense.

If we find people going off the walls, we need to separate ourselves from them. They aren't going to change, to become rational to please us.

Christ came to fulfill God's plan for humanity.

We must stay focused on our plan to achieve our goals.

Distractions can't be allowed. Moving forward is our only option. People who don't want to move with us are against us, and they don't deserve our attention.

Our focus on Christ moves us into the future, and that's where our success will be found.

— Day 72 —

"Always remember to keep your priorities in check. All it takes is forgetting once what comes first in your life to lose all that is dear to you."

◀| *Luke 12:34* |▶

For where your treasure is, there will your heart be also.

Frustration.

A word spoken in anger.

Things can skew out of line just that quickly. A business connection is broken. A marriage crumbles. Our children no longer call.

It's easy to be too focused on one thing and to forget there are people traveling at our side. They deserve our attention in a considerate way.

What's our focus? What's our goal? Do we want to be rich more than we want to be kind?

Is financial wealth the only worthy goal?

Aim high. There's nothing wrong with that. Just don't let that goal become blinders that keep us from seeing what God has already given us.

— Day 73 —

"The greatest opposition to success will be your own inhibitions and doubts."

◀   Titus 2:7-8   ▶

Show yourself in all respects to be a model of good works, and in your teaching show integrity, dignity, and sound speech that cannot be condemned, so that an opponent may be put to shame, having nothing evil to say about us.

Self-doubt can be instilled with unwarranted criticism.

Our inhibitions can become embedded in us when we fail to gain approval from others. Perhaps we had a rough childhood, or other events have broken our sense of self-worth.

We can begin our repair by *doing things in the best possible manner*. We want others to find our actions so commendable that they are unable to fault us.

We must perform our duties with integrity, dignity, and well-spoken words.

We must live as unto God. He will encourage, strengthen, and urge us forward. He will be our greatest asset to finding our confidence and moving into our successful future.

— Day 74 —

"Don't let anger consume you; all it will do is take you to a place you don't want to go."

◀◀   *James 1:19*   ▶▶

Know this, my beloved brothers: let every person be quick to hear, slow to speak, slow to anger.

We are hard-wired for emotions.

Love is one we admire and respect. What about anger?

Should we cast it aside? Is it an evil thing? Of course not. It's part of who we are, human.

There's a key to keeping anger in its place. We find it in the book of James in the Word of God.

1. We are to listen to others before we respond. Sincerely listen and understand what they say.
2. We can't respond back impulsively. We must consider our responses carefully.
3. We must not let anger control us. Words spoken in anger are difficult to retrieve.

When we keep anger at bay, we'll find there's another way.

— Day 75 —

"Don't act hastily or your path will be wrought with mistakes."

◀︎   *Proverbs 19:2*   ▶︎

Desire without knowledge is not good, and whoever makes haste with his feet misses his way.

It's easy to think everyone should enjoy the same level of success. We deserve the corner office just as much as anyone else.

Perhaps we do, but do we know how hard our associate worked for what he or she's achieved? Are we willing to do the same?

We can't go chasing our dreams unprepared. Just because we want it doesn't mean we're ready to achieve it. It's called jumping the gun. To act prematurely. To be hasty, rash, or ahead of oneself.

Preparation is a learning process. It's how we garner understanding and learn the ropes.

It's how we're successful when we do move on up to the success we deserve. If we get there too fast, our feet might miss the way, and we'll tumble right off and lose everything.

— Day 76 —

"There is always a choice."

◀   John 6:44   ▶

No one can come to me unless the Father who sent me draws him.
And I will raise him up on the last day.

Our future comes down to one thing: What do we want out of life?

We try to make it complicated, but it's not. Every decision we make branches into possibilities. We can't always retrace our steps and start over, but we always have a choice.

Attend counseling, or call a divorce lawyer.

Live in a smaller house, or drive a cheaper car.

Work longer hours, or spend time with the kids.

Our choices aren't always easy, but we get to make them. Choosing Christ is always a good option. When He walks at our side, our focus on Him will build our connections to others.

Even when bad things seem to assault us, our choice must be to move forward into our coming success.

— Day 77 —

"Fight only the battles that are going to make a substantive difference."

◀| *Exodus 14:14* |▶

The Lord will fight for you, and you have only to be silent.

Who would argue over the price of gum? Or whether we should toast our bread on one side or two?

Yet, people speak words of anger over such things. Does it matter who fuels the car? Does it hurt us to wait a few moments for the copy machine? Does the yard have to be edged every time we mow?

Then there are the bigger battles, where our company is under fire, perhaps in a hostile takeover. Maybe our neighborhood needs a new elementary school, or a park was vandalized.

We should ask ourselves, will this conflict still be important in five years? What about in ten? If not, let it go, even if it affects our pocketbook, our choice of employer, or where we attend church.

If our core values aren't in peril, then our battle is about pride and needs to be set aside.

— Day 78 —

"Learn at least one new thing every day.
Always continue to expand your
knowledge."

◀   *Proverbs 18:15*   ▶

An intelligent heart acquires knowledge, and the ear of the wise
seeks knowledge.

Stagnant water stinks.

That may seem like an odd statement to start today, but think about it. Water that's not moving allows impurities to multiply and fester, and it becomes putrid with decay.

Our minds are much the same. It's keeping the information in our heads in constant motion that allows us to remain vibrant and sharp.

Read a magazine, either paper or digital.

Work a crossword.

Comment to the editor on a news article.

Discuss a current event with a friend over the phone.

New knowledge gives *new life*, and *knowledge* leads to *success*.

— Day 79 —

"There is no excuse for not moving forward in life."

◀ *James 2:14* ▶

What good is it, my brothers, if someone says he has faith but does not have works? Can that faith save him?

Faith without action is useless.

That sounds harsh, but it's the truth of the hardworking and successful person.

No matter how much we believe in what's important to us, if we're sitting on our sofa and wishing for success, we'll never have it.

Never.

It won't knock on our door and give us this week's Powerball numbers. It just won't.

We need to read Success-Speak daily, pound the pavement with our ideas, aid those who are without help, and put wings to our commitment to Christ and our fellow humans.

We must act on our faith, revealing it by our works.

— Day 80 —

*"If you see and do nothing, you have
chosen not to act. The responsibility is
yours."*

◀   *1 Timothy 5:8*   ▶

*But if anyone does not provide for his relatives, and especially for
members of his household, he has denied the faith and is worse than
an unbeliever.*

We have a responsibility to one another.

John Donne wrote in 1624 that no man is an island. His
words were prescient. Since that time, the world has become
more and more accessible through transportation and media.

At the same time, it's become easier to isolate ourselves
behind our computers, air-conditioned cars, and through online
purchasing.

We've become me-first, and no one else matters.

God's Word says otherwise. If we proclaim Christian values
and forget to put others before ourselves, we've made a mockery
of Christ and His heart for the hurting and downtrodden.

Our goal is easier to reach when we don't go it alone.

— Day 81 —

*"You have a choice in life. You can either
run or you can overcome what you fear."*

◀   Psalm 56:3-4   ▶

*When I am afraid, I put my trust in you. In God, whose word I
praise, in God I trust; I shall not be afraid. What can flesh do to
me?*

Fear is a survival mechanism.

It's an essential part of keeping us safe. It tells us to respond
to danger by either standing up and fighting or turning tail and
running. When we let fear control our actions, we'll run every
time, and we'll never defeat what tries to come against us.

Is your company downsizing? Take a class to learn new skills.

Failing investments? Reinvent your portfolio to focus on
money-makers.

Health issues? Change doctors as many times as necessary.

Our lives are ours to manage. Fear tries to take that away.
When we place our trust in God, we're already moving the correct direction.

— Day 82 —

"You must remember that for every new thing you acquire, a price will be paid, whether in money, time, or relationships."

◀   John 1:14   ▶

And the Word became flesh and dwelt among us, and we have seen his glory, glory as of the only Son from the Father, full of grace and truth.

Jesus came to earth to start His life as a baby in a manger.

He ended it dying on a cross in the worst possible agony.

Yet, He became the preeminent connection uniting God with man, and He is still revered today.

Whatever we gain costs us something. What's most important to us determines what we're willing to pay.

We get none of it for free.

Set your goals high, but be aware of the cost. Choose wisely, but commit wholeheartedly.

Our spiritual choice must be Christ and Christ alone.

We will reach our goal with Him at our side.

— Day 83 —

"Stand tall, walk straight, and be unafraid."

◄   Psalm 112:7   ►

He is not afraid of bad news; his heart is firm, trusting in the LORD.

With *right* comes *might*.

To make that clearer, when we stand on the side of honesty and truth, it empowers us with a boldness that deceitfulness cannot strip away.

We can hold our head high, because our ducks are all aligned.

In our careers, that means we haven't walked over people to get to the top.

In our families, we've shown love and consideration to those sharing our roof.

In our church, we've lived as unto the Lord.

We become the good news that people can trust. We walk unafraid when God is on our side.

— Day 84 —

*"A choice stands before you. You can
either sit idly by while the world changes
and have no control. Or you can make a
stand and be the one changing the world."*

◀   *Ephesians 6:13*   ▶

*Therefore take up the whole armor of God, that you may be able to
withstand in the evil day, and having done all, to stand firm.*

A soldier makes a choice every day. He picks up his weapon
and goes into battle, or he doesn't.

He watches the war rage without him, or he changes the
outcome with his gut and determination.

You may think, a soldier? There's no choice there. He's
required to follow orders, to risk life and limb.

True, but it started with a choice to become a part, and every
day he makes a choice to participate, whatever the consequences.

Have we made our choice? Are we on the sideline, or are we
willing to join the battle?

We won't change the world until we choose to act. We fight
our battle with preparation, knowledge, and trust in God to lead
us into success.

— Day 85 —

"Success comes from hard work, faith, and the confidence to utilize the opportunities that come across your path."

◀︎ Proverbs 3:26 ▶︎

For the LORD will be your confidence and will keep your foot from being caught.

Success: a desired outcome, whether financial or social

Hard work: to give extra effort above what's required

Faith: a level of trust that leaves no room for doubt

Confidence: to be absolutely convinced

We plan for the first, do the second, have the third, and build the fourth. How? By taking advantage of every opportunity that comes our way.

Opportunity: favorable circumstances

It's called striking when the iron is hot. We take advantage of the situation without infringing on others' rights or doing harm to ourselves.

The Lord will be our confidence when we follow Him.

— Day 86 —

"What do you really want out of life? Is it really just financial success, or is it happiness—the satisfaction and joy of a complete life?"

◂❙   Ecclesiastes 3:12   ❙▸

I perceived that there is nothing better for them than to be joyful and to do good as long as they live.

Having money may be better than not, but it doesn't ensure happiness.

Without good friends, good health, and a good environment, we'll be miserable, no matter the size of our bank account.

Steve Jobs, founder of the Apple corporation, became immensely wealthy. His biographer, Walter Isaacson, recorded his regret at the end of his life:

"I wanted my kids to know me [and] I wasn't always there for them."

If we have little joy aside from work, it's time to rethink our goals. Just having financial success creates a shell that's filled with emptiness.

We fill our shell by *doing good for as long as we live.*

— Day 87 —

"Listen to the advice of those around you, but take to heart what your instincts tell you to do."

◀ Proverbs 11:14 ▶

Where there is no guidance, a people falls, but in an abundance of counselors there is safety.

Even the President has advisors. When they know what they're doing, the Commander-in-Chief is successful. When they don't, he stumbles.

At times, those in power need to stand on their own instincts, whether to go one way or the other. Otherwise, they become followers rather than leaders, and they no longer command respect.

John F. Kennedy is famous for taking the advice of his generals—against his better judgment—when he first entered office, resulting in the disastrous Bay of Pigs invasion of Cuba.

His lesson learned? Kennedy vowed he would trust his own instincts in military matters from that day forward.

We should listen to our advisors but act in the way that is right for us. When we trust in God, we'll find guidance in Him.

— Day 88 —

*"Asking for help is not a sign of weakness;
it's a sign of wisdom."*

◀   *Proverbs 19:20*   ▶

*Listen to advice and accept instruction, that you may gain wisdom
in the future.*

My way or the highway.

It's a strong-minded person who thinks that way. He or she often doesn't work well with other people.

Studies show us that the most successful people in business aren't those who are the brightest, but rather the ones who are willing to collaborate. Sharing knowledge makes people smarter. It's not weakness. It's good management.

Here's the thing, though. Once we ask for advice, we can't discount what we've learned. If we pick and choose from the advice we're given, on the basis of whether it suits us or not, then we're back to "my way or the highway," no matter how nicely we say it.

Let's put our heads together. When we're looking forward, together we'll find success just down the road.

— Day 89 —

"Any goal, any objective is possible . . . at a cost."

◀   2 *Timothy* 2:15   ▶

Do your best to present yourself to God as one approved, a worker who has no need to be ashamed, rightly handling the word of truth.

How hard are we willing to work for what's important to us?

Is four years of college too much to ask? Six? Some degrees require us to attend even longer.

What if no one is willing to pay our tuition and fees? How much are we willing to borrow?

All the options are open to us . . . if we're willing to do whatever it takes.

CEO? Certainly, you can have it.

President? The time to start is now.

Evangelist? Move into your dream.

We must get started, work continually, and never look back. Our success is on the way.

— Day 90 —

*"Do not let your fear of loss inhibit your
ability to succeed."*

◀ Psalm 34:17-20 ▮▶

*When the righteous cry for help, the LORD hears and delivers them
out of all their troubles. The LORD is near to the brokenhearted
and saves the crushed in spirit. Many are the afflictions of the
righteous, but the LORD delivers him out of them all. He keeps all
his bones; not one of them is broken.*

We can't lose what we don't already have.

Success is our goal. We reach for it with an outstretched
hand. We miss it when we let our fears chain our feet to the past.

We can't afford to focus on what might be lost, but must
keep our sights on what we might accomplish. The future is filled
with possibilities. When we're in motion; and our face is pointed
forward; and our reverse gear is disengaged, we will find success.

When we struggle (and we will from time to time) we can
count on our Lord to lift us into His consolation, so that we can
be strengthened and continue to pursue our goals.

The Lord is near the brokenhearted, and He is there for us.

— Day 91 —

"Your primary path to failure is to give in to defeat."

◀| Psalm 73:26 |▶

My flesh and my heart may fail, but God is the strength of my heart and my portion forever.

If we take a wrong turn, we might lose our destination.

In a travel series, the hosts were in Japan. Their car's GPS was in Japanese, and the written and spoken prompts were in the local language. The hosts could only follow the onscreen arrows.

They wound up on a closed-off mountain highway with no clue how to find their destination.

Frustration mounted until they began to turn their car around. The map on their GPS immediately reset, rerouting them an alternate direction.

We reset ourselves in moments of trouble by getting back on the highway. If we do nothing, we've already accepted our defeat.

Move forward. Find a new path. Reset yourself with determination to achieve your goal.

— Day 92 —

"Seek and hold onto the living Word of
God with all your strength."

◀   Jeremiah 23:29   ▶

Is not my word like fire, declares the LORD, and like a hammer
that breaks the rock in pieces?

Soft metal is good to no one.

Buy a cheap screw, apply force with the screwdriver, and you'll strip the head.

A weak link on a chain will break under pressure.

Who would build a car out of aluminum foil?

Tools are better when they're formed from hardened carbon steel. A good hammer made of high-quality metal can crush rock all day long.

When we study the Bible and pull the truth from its pages, and we implement it into our lives, we hold the hammer of God, and it will crush all opposition.

With God's Word, we'll move into our success, stepping forward and clearing our path as we go.

— Day 93 —

"Your understanding is limited by what you allow it to be."

◀   Proverbs 4:7   ▶

The beginning of wisdom is this: Get wisdom, and whatever you get, get insight.

Insight is defined as the ability to see into a situation, to be able to understand the nature of what's happening around us, without needing to have it explained in detail.

We understand the reality of what's occurring, because it makes sense to us.

That doesn't mean we think it's sensible, but we see how to work though the matter, to bring things to a conclusion, perhaps even how to turn the situation around to our best interest.

Insight doesn't come all at once. A tenth-year teacher might understand student confrontations that would mystify a newbie. A banker with experience can spot the flaws in a bad loan from a mile away. The seasoned Christian knows when sin rides too closely, and it's time to step back.

Wisdom can be learned, and with it, insight will take us far.

— Day 94 —

*"Set a goal today, one that is further than
you have ever achieved before."*

◄| *Genesis 12:1* |►

*Now the LORD said to Abram, "Go from your country and your
kindred and your father's house to the land that I will show you."*

Abraham was a mighty man of God. We see him as the great
believer, the one that God would use to change the world, and
he was.

First, though, he had to get out of his comfort zone.

Our comfort zone might be financial, or it might be the
people around us. Some people find their comfort in food,
alcohol, or television.

Maybe we're couch potatoes, and the idea of working for a
living depresses us.

We won't find our success on our couch, or anywhere else in
our comfort zone. It's called a goal for a reason. It's just out of
reach, and we must stretch to get there. Once we reach it, we set
a new goal that's even further ahead. Let's get moving and see
what God has in store for us.

— Day 95 —

"Understand that you may not be the only person attempting to achieve your goals. Act soon before the opportunity goes to someone else."

◄   *Ephesians 5:15-16*   ►

Look carefully then how you walk, not as unwise but as wise, making the best use of the time, because the days are evil.

Have you ever had a really great idea, and before you could put it into play, someone else did?

Take the personal computer.

They had computers already, but someone had a great idea, *acted on it,* and today, we have Microsoft.

Then there's Amazon, Facebook, and a hundred others.

Elon Musk took an idea over a hundred years old and built a car company of electric vehicles, Tesla. Soon, all the automotive manufacturers were jumping on board, but Musk stole the show. He was the first to do it right and do it bigger than life.

Go big or go home. That's a sports mantra that drives many clubs and teams. We should take it for our own. We must jump in wholeheartedly, or our success will forever be out of our reach.

— Day 96 —

*"Don't let fear stand in the way of
achieving your potential."*

◀︎   *Matthew 14:27*   ▶︎

*But immediately Jesus spoke to them, saying, "Take heart; it is I.
Do not be afraid."*

Fear is the mind killer.

It strips our confidence from us, and we can't move forward
into the success we want to find.

We must take Jesus' words to heart: "Do not be afraid."

We do this one step at a time. We test the water, and we take
courage in our small success. Then we step fully out of the boat,
until we're chasing after our goal.

Run on the water, swim in the sea, or use the motor in the
boat, just go and go fast, so your dream doesn't get away.

If we get a little wet along the way, that's just fear speaking.
Take heart. Our Lord is with us, and we'll find our strength
through our faith in Him.

We can't let anything stand in the way of our success.

— Day 97 —

"Don't falter when obstacles appear in your path. With perseverance, they will be overcome and success will be yours."

◀︎   *Hebrews 12:1*   ▶︎

Therefore, since we are surrounded by so great a cloud of witnesses, let us also lay aside every weight, and sin which clings so closely, and let us run with endurance the race that is set before us.

Life is an obstacle course.

It's like walking through your house at night after the kids have been up late. You're going to find that plastic block with your bare feet. Just expect it, because that's the way it is.

Financial punches will knock us for a loop. Marital knots will fray our emotions. Our children will have days we'll wonder if they're sane.

That's the spice of life, what makes the human experience special. Don't give up. Work around and through the things that block us from our goal.

We're running an Olympic hurdle. When we leap every obstacle, the gold medal will be ours. We will stand on the podium in the winner's place, and our victory will taste sweet.

— Day 98 —

"Don't let regret hold you back from the future you can have or the success you can achieve."

◀ᛁ   Isaiah 43:18-19   ᛁ▶

Remember not the former things, nor consider the things of old. Behold, I am doing a new thing; now it springs forth, do you not perceive it? I will make a way in the wilderness and rivers in the desert.

Each day is a walled garden, with a gate at either end.

We must leave our garden with the sunset to enter another at the rising of the sun.

We can never return. We can't water or prune except in today's garden.

What grows (or doesn't) in yesterday's garden is out of our control.

Tomorrow's garden is hidden behind a closed door, inaccessible.

God will make a way for us to find our success. Yesterday isn't ours to worry about. We must garden in the day we have.

— Day 99 —

*"Don't let tomorrow be the same as today.
Reach out, push forward, and make
progress."*

◀ *Philippians 1:9* ▶

*And it is my prayer that your love may abound more and more,
with knowledge and all discernment.*

Take two stones, one from a stagnant pond, and the other from a tumbling stream.

Which is beautiful to behold?

The stone from the pond has had an easy life, but it will be jagged and mossy, and unpleasant to the touch.

The one from the stream has been polished by the water, and it's shiny and smooth. We want to hold it in our hand.

Every day, we sit in a pond and stagnate, or life rushes around us, pummeling our rough edges. If it does, we become beautiful to the touch, and people want to hold us in their hands.

Progress comes from the new and unfamiliar. We might have to fight, be tumbled about, and get a few rough spots smoothed away, but our beauty comes when we reach our goal.

— Day 100 —

"How you choose to spend your time is a
key definition of your character."

◄| *Proverbs 10:9* |►

Whoever walks in integrity walks securely, but he who makes his
ways crooked will be found out.

How's our volunteer list looking?

What have we done *for free* without being coerced into giving
our time?

We're defined by what we do. Integrity in our private time
tells more about us than our public face ever will.

It's our backyard behavior that tells the world who we are.

Changing your character happens when you change how you
spend your time. Sign up for that committee. Work the extra job.
Be as diligent at home as you are at work.

Be the person your employer expects you to be, your family
needs you to be, and your God hopes you will be.

When our character is defined by success, it will be written
in everything we say and do.

— Day 101 —

*"Continually increasing your knowledge
equates to the furthering and expanding
of the horizons before you."*

◀   Isaiah 11:2   ▶

*And the Spirit of the LORD shall rest upon him, the Spirit of
wisdom and understanding, the Spirit of counsel and might, the
Spirit of knowledge and the fear of the LORD.*

It's said that the best way to write well is to read often. The greater our exposure to new information, the broader the concepts to which we have access.

In other words, the more we know, the more we become aware of life's opportunities.

Following Christ broadens our horizons in six ways. We receive wisdom, understanding, counsel, might, knowledge, and fear (respect).

That's the unqualified definition of a successful person in anyone's book. We'll make right decisions through the insight we've gained through our preparation for our upcoming success.

All doors are open to us when Christ is our mentor and guide.

— Day 102 —

*"Without the belief that you can achieve
your goals, it is unlikely that you ever
will."*

◄| *Matthew 28:19* |►

*Go therefore and make disciples of all nations, baptizing them in
the name of the Father and of the Son and of the Holy Spirit.*

The difficult thing is the one that frustrates us.

Erik Weihenmayer was the first blind person to reach the top
of Mount Everest. It was a difficult task, impossible in most
people's eyes, yet he was determined. Erik believed he could reach
the summit, and he did.

There are no barriers, when we believe in our goals. A new
business? Started! A university degree? Done! Travel around the
world? Yes, you can do it!

If you don't believe it can be done, it won't be. When you
step out on your faith, you'll reach the goal you desire, and you'll
be there before you know it.

Erik started small and stretched his limits with each new
climb. We can follow his example and reach our Mount Everest,
one steady ascent at a time.

— Day 103 —

"Seek out not how to win but how to succeed."

1 Corinthians 13:1-3   ▶

If I speak in the tongues of men and of angels, but have not love, I am a noisy gong or a clanging cymbal. And if I have prophetic powers, and understand all mysteries and all knowledge, and if I have all faith, so as to remove mountains, but have not love, I am nothing. If I give away all I have, and if I deliver up my body to be burned, but have not love, I gain nothing.

Winning gives us power over others.

Yet, true success comes in a different way.

What fills us with contentment? What outcome do we desire from our lives? Do we want plenty of money? Our grandchildren nearby? A successful game of golf? A music career? Or perhaps to retire early?

What will it take for us to get there? If we forget the important stuff along the way, we might win, but we won't succeed. Paul says it this way: "If I have not love . . ."

It's a lesson everyone should learn.

— Day 104 —

"You must believe in your success."

Romans 10:10   ▶

For with the heart one believes and is justified, and with the mouth one confesses and is saved.

Try this experiment: Say, "I'm useless and pathetic," three times. Repeat it like you mean it.

How does it make you feel?

Now do the opposite. "I am successful." Then list several ways you've been successful.

How does *that* make you feel? Better?

What we say affects our outlook on our situation. If our bank account dips, say aloud, "It'll replenish when I get my paycheck." If we argue with our spouse, genuinely include the words, "I love you." If we struggle, look to Success-Speak for inspiration.

When we believe we're successful—in any area of our life—and we *say it aloud,* our circumstances will change, and everyone around us will notice the difference.

— Day 105 —

"Preparation is key to achieving your goals and being successful."

◀ Proverbs 6:6-8 ▶

Go to the ant, O sluggard; consider her ways, and be wise. Without having any chief, officer, or ruler, she prepares her bread in summer and gathers her food in harvest.

Do you have a list of goals for the rest of your life?

Try this: Prepare an agenda of where you want to be in five years, ten, and then twenty. Then ask yourself, what steps will it take to get there?

Post your goals and your steps, and under each one, write down one thing you can do to actively make it happen.

What can you *do*, in *measurable action*, to *achieve your plan?*

The tiny ant doesn't go outside in October, look around, and say, "I guess I should begin to prepare." This marvel of industry is preparing all summer long.

Our summer is on us. It's time to take our first step on the path to our goal. The moment to begin our success is now.

— Day 106 —

"Neither fear nor bravado is always the correct choice, and wisdom is knowing when to flee or to hold your ground."

◀︎   *James 3:17*   ▶︎

But the wisdom from above is first pure, then peaceable, gentle, open to reason, full of mercy and good fruits, impartial and sincere.

An experienced soldier knows when a position is defensible.

A capable mediator can tell when one side needs to give in to another.

There are times it's important to bail out of financial ventures. Otherwise, we'll lose our shirt and go bankrupt.

We can be afraid of what might happen, or we can run roughshod over wise advice to get our way.

Wisdom from God says there's a better way.

We must be pure, peaceable, gentle, open to reason, full of mercy and good fruits (good deeds), impartial and sincere.

Man's wisdom says to make the choice that's best for us. God's wisdom directs us to make the choice that's best for others.

— Day 107 —

"Understand the past, but do not dwell in it."

◀   *Ecclesiastes 1:9*   ▶

What has been is what will be, and what has been done is what will be done, and there is nothing new under the sun.

We build out of stone if we want something to last.

Yet, even stone is impermanent. Water is a fluid substance, and given time, it can wear away the toughest rock.

When we understand the properties of stone and water, we know how best to use them. Dealing with the past is the same.

History is already written, immovable and impermeable. What's done is finished, and we must move on.

We can't change it by wishing or worrying.

To move into our success, we must move into our future. We must cast aside the stones of the past, and leap into the opportunities awaiting us.

Your success is expecting you. Get out and achieve it.

— Day 108 —

"Much may stand in your path, but if you allow success to be your only option, then success you will find."

◀   Luke 16:10-11   ▶

One who is faithful in a very little is also faithful in much, and one who is dishonest in a very little is also dishonest in much. If then you have not been faithful in the unrighteous wealth, who will entrust to you the true riches?

Where does our successful behavior start?

When we win the lottery? When our bank accounts reach a million bucks? No, this is it: When we move into a big house and buy a sports car.

Nope. Not it.

Our successful behavior starts today, no matter where we stand financially. We help others, even when we have nothing. We claim God's goodness, even when we can't see it in our life.

We are faithful to God and our goals in the little things, so that we can learn to be faithful when success sweeps over us.

To be truly effective, we need to practice our success now.

— Day 109 —

"You can be the one shaping the world;
you just can't let fear stand in your way."

◀ *Proverbs 29:25* ▶

The fear of man lays a snare, but whoever trusts in the LORD is
safe.

The big question is the elephant in the room.

What's stopping you from reaching your goal?

Where has your confidence gone?

Are the people around you bringing you down? Are they slowing your progress toward your goal?

It's your world, your life, and your decision. Other people might not want your success as much as you do.

Step out anyway. Move forward without them, if you must. Chase your goal with all the tenacity you can manage.

You will be a world-changer. You have the desire. Now it's time to take that next step.

The Lord at your side will be your guide. Trust in Him.

— Day 110 —

"The choice to be successful is yours and not based upon where you grew up, your education, your life previous to this point, or who people say you are."

◀   *Galatians 5:1*   ▶

For freedom Christ has set us free; stand firm therefore, and do not submit again to a yoke of slavery.

Anything that restricts us keeps us enslaved. Lack of education, family circumstances, or strained resources, all can be shackles on our attempts to make our mark in life.

We are free from those things when we choose to be free.

We can find a new life in Christ, and our old self is renewed in Him. It works spiritually, and it's equally successful in the physical world.

We might face a tight month financially, but that's just slavery talking, trying to lock us up once again.

Is our family bringing us down? No! We won't allow it!

Not even our lack of education is a conflict. We can resource those skills from the workforce or the Internet.

We need to make a choice to find our success now!

— Day 111 —

*"One person's version of success may not
be the same as yours. Ask yourself what
you really desire."*

◀◁   *Psalm 37:4*   ▷▶

*Delight yourself in the LORD, and he will give you the desires of
your heart.*

The job of advertisers in America's economy is to convince
us we want things we don't even know exist.

We must have them, we're told, because they are vital,
socially acceptable, and will give us happiness.

We're not told that mankind survived just fine for the previous hundred years without it. That's not part of the sales pitch.
That doesn't *convince you to purchase the product.*

Much of our purchasing is driven by comparison to those
around us. We call it keeping up with the Joneses. If they get a
new car, we must have one. Swimming pools, vacation homes,
and big screen televisions. There's no end to the list.

Success should be personal. When we're true to ourselves and
our Lord in heaven, we'll find our success is easier to find than
ever before.

— Day 112 —

"Make the choice that you know is the correct decision and not just what people tell you is right."

◀   1 John 4:18   ▶

There is no fear in love, but perfect love casts out fear. For fear has to do with punishment, and whoever fears has not been perfected in love.

Fear is like riding in a submarine in the depths of the ocean. Just one crack in the hull, and the ocean rushes in.

If we've set our goal, and naysayers try to distract us, they are pushing our submarine under the water's surface. The more they jabber on, the farther underwater we find ourselves.

The moment we begin to listen, that's when the doubt rushes in. Our faith in our choice becomes cracked, and we will drown.

When people care about us, they'll support our goals. They'll lift us up and set us on firm ground, so that we can strike out once more toward our goal.

Christ is our example and our supporter. He loves us, and we need have no fear. Today, our ship rises to the surface, through our faith in Him.

— Day 113 —

"Don't let excuses stand in your way of success."

◁ *Luke 14:18-20* ▷

But they all alike began to make excuses. The first said to him, 'I have bought a field, and I must go out and see it. Please have me excused.' And another said, 'I have bought five yoke of oxen, and I go to examine them. Please have me excused.' And another said, 'I have married a wife, and therefore I cannot come.'

What's your excuse for not reaching your goal?

What? You don't have one? Or do you think your excuse is not an excuse at all, but a reason that's really good?

Anything that keeps you from your success is an excuse, plain and simple. Cast it off. Get around it. Get out the chainsaw and get to clearing the way.

Whatever's in the way will keep you from your success if you let it. God doesn't listen to our excuses. Instead, He says, "Let's get going!"

— Day 114 —

"Before committing your life to a goal or objective, you need to ensure that the cost is worth the gain."

No one can serve two masters, for either he will hate the one and love the other, or he will be devoted to the one and despise the other. You cannot serve God and money.

Our goal might be to raise respectful children.

Or to become a rich tycoon.

Or to retire at 30 and never have to work again.

If money's our focus, we can achieve that. The question is, at what cost?

Being a top-notch parent may mean we can't fulfill other goals, such as full-time employment or life-long dreams.

Are we willing to retire at 30 if we must give up our favorite luxuries?

Be careful what you want, because the road we travel to get there will exclude other options from our slate. When it's over and done, will you be glad you chose your goal?

— Day 115 —

"It isn't what the mistake was or how you made it, but instead how you recovered from that mistake and what you learned from the experience."

◀   *James 5:16*   ▶

Therefore, confess your sins to one another and pray for one another, that you may be healed. The prayer of a righteous person has great power as it is working.

Every school boy falls off his bike at least once.

It's not the falling off that's important. It's getting back on and continuing down the street.

If Michael Phelps, Olympic phenomenon, had given in to his attention deficit disorder, he wouldn't have won 23 gold medals.

Keanu Reeves, actor of Matrix fame, was expelled from high school; his father was imprisoned for selling heroin; and his family moved constantly. Today, he has a star on the Hollywood Walk of Fame.

Leave your mistakes behind. They aren't *you.* How you recover is what you become. Aim toward your goal, and it will be yours.

— Day 116 —

"As long as you are moving forward, failure should never be a word in your vocabulary."

◀   *1 Peter 3:18*   ▶

For Christ also suffered once for sins, the righteous for the unrighteous, that he might bring us to God, being put to death in the flesh but made alive in the spirit.

Success steps beyond failure.

The supreme failure is death, right? If we aren't alive, how can we be successful at anything else?

Jesus died on the cross, and He became the biggest success story in history.

Our stumbles can be turned around, corrected, and reinvented. Just because we scraped our knee once is no excuse not to get back up and try again.

It's the work that makes us a success, not the whining about how hard it's been.

If something's in our way, go over, around, or under it. Just get to the other side, and keep aimed toward your goal.

— Day 117 —

"The strength to succeed is multiplied when you have faith in your success to accomplish your goals."

◄   *Luke 1:37*   ►

For nothing will be impossible with God.

The giraffe feeds on the thorny acacia. The thorns are five inches long.

A honey bear endures vicious attacks from the bees to raid the comb.

The sperm whale dives to the bottom of the ocean to feed on deadly giant squid.

Our lack of education? No thorn is too long or too spiny. Faltering finances? They can't sting enough to keep us away. Harsh criticism? Forgotten as if it never happened.

Our strength is MULTIPLIED when we have the confidence we will succeed in our goals. Our faith comes from God, and with ongoing preparation for our success, we will overcome all that's in our way.

Nothing is impossible with God.

— Day 118 —

*"Be brave, stand by all that you've done,
and don't hide from what you can
become."*

◀︎   *Jeremiah 23:23-24*   ▶︎

*Am I a God at hand, declares the LORD, and not a God far away?
Can a man hide himself in secret places so that I cannot see him?
declares the LORD. Do I not fill heaven and earth? declares
the LORD.*

There's nothing hidden in the modern world.

Cameras, microphones, and our web searches. They all reflect an image of who and what we are.

It's time to own up to our past and move forward. What we can become isn't in the recorded memory in some computer facility.

The future is in front of us, waiting on us to break the chains of the past. Yesterday has no hold on us, if we don't let it. We must launch out from our circumstances and trust in God to make us new.

We are capable of so much more than we think. Be brave. Be confident. Take a chance. Grab your goal and never turn loose.

— Day 119 —

"Today, create and formulate a plan to achieve at least one goal."

◄ Psalm 20:4 ►

May he grant you your heart's desire and fulfill all your plans!

Michael Jordon, one of sport's greats, had to learn to walk.

He was a baby one day, and he crawled across the floor. Then, he took one step, and the rest is history.

Billy Graham, often called America's pastor, spoke his first message. It was his moment to take his first step, and he ministered to the world.

Your first step happens today. Did you wash the breakfast dishes? Scrub a toilet? Put gas in the car? You're taking baby steps.

Did you plan something harder, like speaking kindly to the neighbor that complains about your dog?

Choose something you can do, something just out of your comfort zone. That's a success under your belt, and the next time, you can reach a little further.

God holds our hands, and He helps us reach our goals.

— Day 120 —

"If you desire change, then you must be the one to take hold of it and lead it into the open."

◀   *Ecclesiastes 3:1*   ▶

For everything there is a season, and a time for every matter under heaven.

Your season is now.

Today.

Get out of bed. The winds are changing. It's a new season, one of hope and anticipation, a time of sowing and harvest, a day of planting and reaping.

Read your Success-Speak quote daily, take your opportunity by the hand, and step toward your goal. You're the one who makes the decision, not your spouse or your employer. It's not up to the government or the minister of your fellowship.

Your life and your future are on your shoulders.

You must plant before the harvest, but it is on its way.

Reach your hand to the future. Claim it.

— Day 121 —

"There's a difference between what's within your perceived grasp and what is actually within your reach. Don't let yourself be held back."

◀   *John 10:10*   ▶

The thief comes only to steal and kill and destroy. I came that they may have life and have it abundantly.

Our lack of vision starves our creativity.

In other words, when we can't see our goal in our mind's eye, we don't even realize it's there, that it's possible, and that we can achieve it.

We're in a rowboat, in the fog, without a paddle.

And we don't have a foghorn to toot for help.

Jesus opened people's eyes to possibilities. He showed them life could be different. They could step outside their troubled existence and become better. They didn't have to maintain the status quo. They could live in a new and improved situation, and they could share that with others and lift them up to a better future.

That's what our goals are for, lifting not just us, but all of us.

— Day 122 —

"The greatest achievements are those that you accomplish for the Lord."

◀   *1 Corinthians 2:9*   ▮▶

But, as it is written, "What no eye has seen, nor ear heard, nor the heart of man imagined, what God has prepared for those who love him"—

What lasts?

Truly, what will be left when we leave this world behind?

Houses? In the California wildfires of 2017, the iconic Glass House, a stunning $17 million steel-framed structure, was razed by flames in hours. Nothing was left.

Cars? The Houston floods of the same year took out a million cars.

What people will remember from those disasters will be the good their neighbors did, the rescues by First Responders, and help offered from people a thousand miles away.

If we love God, let's live like we do. Our love for our Lord is revealed in the compassion we have for those around us.

— Day 123 —

"You must have a specific goal if you don't want to waste your time and energy reaching for success."

◀   John 6:12   ▶

And when they had eaten their fill, he told his disciples, "Gather up the leftover fragments, that nothing may be lost."

The old saying says to waste not and we'll want not. If our money leaks away like water through a sieve, we'll never achieve our biggest dreams.

What are the holes like in your wallet? Do you review your transactions monthly?

Or do your jeans have ripped and torn pockets, allowing your paycheck to disappear? Can you track where the cash went?

Does your savings account balance equal a big fat zero, nothing more than an empty hole that never gets filled? Does every dime get spent each month?

Jesus said to gather up all the fragments. It's the quarters that count, the leftover cash and the change we toss into the drawer. It's paying attention to the details of our financial life that will lead us to higher levels of success.

— Day 124 —

"Make a goal and don't surrender it."

◂ *James 1:22* ▸

But be doers of the word, and not hearers only, deceiving yourselves.

The biggest failures come from the people who had the biggest dreams and did nothing about them.

Just making a goal does nothing for helping us reach it.

Take a basketball player. He stands at the free-throw line, and it's his opportunity to score a point for the team.

Unless that ball leaves his hand, he'll never score. The crowd can cheer, and he can determine he's making that goal, but until his hands move, nothing's happening.

Our goal is a pipe dream until we act to make it a reality. Then we continue to act until our goal is ours.

Would Christendom have covered the world if the Apostles had looked around, said, "Wouldn't Jesus have loved to speak His message to those hurting people?" and then gone back to their daily lives? Plan! Act! Never surrender your goal!

— Day 125 —

"Don't let the past prevent you from achieving your potential in the future."

◀   *Psalm 71:20*   ▶

You who have made me see many troubles and calamities will revive me again; from the depths of the earth you will bring me up again.

A piton driven into a rock makes a sturdy mooring for a ship.

The breezes can blow, but we're not moving while we're tied up. The ship is fixed in place until the chains are cast aside.

Our past is like that piton. It holds us back from achieving our potential. We can't launch ourselves into the future, if we're moored to the past.

We must disengage, release the chains, and cast off.

The Bible tells us God will bring us up again, no matter how low we've fallen. The Father doesn't let our past prevent us from being used for Him.

We can't allow it, either. The future is our promise, and it's out there waiting on us. Ready, set, sail.

— Day 126 —

"Commitment is required to achieve your goals."

◀   Luke 9:62   ▶

Jesus said to him, "No one who puts his hand to the plow and looks back is fit for the kingdom of God."

Butterfly Christians.

They flutter from church to church, and preacher to preacher, hoping to find someplace that suits their fancy.

Until they set down roots, they never will.

Our future grows from our investment in our goals. It doesn't spring into place in full bloom.

We plant a garden in the spring in faith that we will have a harvest come fall. If we plow it up every other week, we'll never manage a successful crop.

What are you aiming for? Keep at it, eyes focused, and let nothing distract you. Not new cars, a trip to the mall, or a weekend with your friends.

Your goal will be yours only when you stick to your plan.

— Day 127 —

"If you can't stand proudly by all that you've done, then it's time to make a difference in how you live your life."

Philippians 2:16   ▶

Holding fast to the word of life, so that in the day of Christ I may be proud that I did not run in vain or labor in vain.

What if our tombstone was a video screen?

Passersby could tap it and see any part of our life.

Are there parts we'd want to change? If so, now's our chance. This morning. Today, before the sun goes down.

If we go to the theater and watch a movie, the ending is what we take away from it. If the beginning is slow or clumsily made, but the final scenes are exciting, that's what we'll discuss on the way home.

"Did you see . . ." or "I was so amazed when . . ."

That's the life we want to live. When the mourners leave our funeral, we want them to say, "Can you believe all the good he did?"

Let's start our change today.

— Day 128 —

"Do not act rashly; for with such actions come mistakes."

◀   Proverbs 17:28   ▶

Even a fool who keeps silent is considered wise; when he closes his lips, he is deemed intelligent.

We tell stories about the wise old owl. From the Iliad to Winnie the Pooh, this wide-eyed bird earns our respect.

It turns out that the wise old owl is no more than an illusion. The owl's wisdom is simply a blank look. The animal is no smarter than many birds, and in fact, falls into the lower realm of bird intelligence.

If the owl could speak, we'd know that immediately.

What do our actions say about us? Do our well-thought-out responses speak highly of us, or do we open our mouths and prove our worst fears, that we are fools who don't deserve to be at the table?

Whether in business, our personal relationships, or in our connection with God, think, let it rest overnight, then approach difficult problems. With a clear head, the answer will be obvious.

— Day 129 —

"To instigate change we must act on what
we know is right."

◀ *James 2:17* ▶

So also faith by itself, if it does not have works, is dead.

A lightbulb is easy to change.

Anyone can do it. Unscrew the bulb and put the new one in.

Yet, what happens when the bulb is situated in a difficult location? Perhaps on a second-story landing, or behind the dash in the car?

It's easy to look at it, wish for it to be changed, and not do anything about it. Someone will, just not us.

The fact is, the bulb won't get changed until we get out the ladder (or screwdriver) and get busy.

We must get into action. Just hoping won't change a thing.

It takes our hand on the bulb and our arm removing it from the socket.

Have faith in your goal, but act on achieving it today.

— Day 130 —

"Understand, learn, and continue forward."

◀   *Hebrews 10:26*   ▶

For if we go on sinning deliberately after receiving the knowledge of the truth, there no longer remains a sacrifice for sins.

A farmer plows his first furrow by line of sight.

He sets his eye on an object—a tree, a fencepost, or a large rock—and he watches it constantly to keep his furrow straight.

If he looks away, he'll go off course, and it will affect every other row in the field.

Our eye must remain on our goal. Locked in. Never wavering.

If we look away, it will affect every other part of our life.

Stay locked on your goal, whatever it is. Family, a new business, or independence from debt. Study to prepare yourself, learn all you can, and keep making headway toward your destination.

The rest of your life will fall in line when you're focused on where you want to go, and one day, your goal will be yours.

— Day 131 —

"Being patient will change your life in a profound way."

◄|　　　2 Peter 3:9　　　|►

The Lord is not slow to fulfill his promise as some count slowness, but is patient toward you, not wishing that any should perish, but that all should reach repentance.

Interior designers know a truth about furnishing a new home. It takes time to have the needed items custom built. And they don't always arrive when we want.

So, do we go out and buy a new sofa, when our custom-ordered one is on the way and held up for an extra week?

Or do we insist the designer paint the living room a color we won't like simply to get it done?

If we do, we won't be happy. We must wait on our promised design to come together. Our patience will yield a better result.

We can't force the promises of the Lord. We can't rush reaching our goal. We can't set aside our preparation for tomorrow just to make something easier for today. Our goal is just out there. Stay on the mark, be patient, and it will be ours.

— Day 132 —

"Success is measured not by how far you traveled, but by how well you traveled."

◀   *Proverbs 3:23*   ▶

Then you will walk on your way securely, and your foot will not stumble.

Traveling in Cadillac style.

That has very little to do with the car we drive, but, rather, with how we live our lives.

It's in our decisions and the quality of our choices. It's seen in the people we associate with, the places we go, and the way we choose to spend our free time.

Here's a good way to determine if someone's traveling in Cadillac style: How many friends show up when they have a pool party? How many birthday wishes do they get on social media? When a disaster happens to them, can we even count the people who come to offer aid?

We can be rich and not figure out Cadillac living. We can be poor and enjoy the luxury of people who love us and sincerely wish us the best in everything we do.

— Day 133 —

"Success is solely based upon whether you make the choice to succeed and are willing to make the necessary sacrifices to achieve success."

Philippians 2:17   ▶

Even if I am to be poured out as a drink offering upon the sacrificial offering of your faith, I am glad and rejoice with you all.

The most successful men and women in the world have given up something.

Perhaps it's anonymity, the chance to walk to Starbucks to have a coffee on a Saturday morning.

Or maybe it's time at the lake on a fall afternoon, just to watch the leaves glisten in the breeze.

Our price for success is very personal. Our children, raised by a nanny or their parents? College, four years or eight? Drive that expensive car now or invest in our business venture?

Our success is determined by our choices. We make them in the small ways before the world sees them in the large ones.

Skip the luxury latte. Pinch the pennies. Do what it takes. You'll find your success.

— Day 134 —

*"Show the path to those who need to see
it. Those that are wandering, lost, and
without direction need assistance to get
their life together and to begin making
advancements."*

◀   Luke 15:20   ▶

*And he arose and came to his father. But while he was still a long
way off, his father saw him and felt compassion, and ran and
embraced him and kissed him.*

Today's verse is from the story of The Prodigal Son.

The young man went off to squander his share of the family
inheritance in wild living. He wasted everything and was reduced
to living with the pigs.

When he returned, broken, his father welcomed him with
open arms.

Who do we know that's wandered off? Maybe they've strayed
financially, and they struggle to pay their bills? Or emotionally,
and they've fallen into an abusive situation?

Maybe it's a matter of someone who's inexperienced, and we
can be his or her mentor. It will take time and effort, but it's our
duty to return what we've been given to those who need it most.
God gave His Son unto us. How can we not give back for Him?

— Day 135 —

"Watch out for the fallacies of others and their personal agendas. Just remember that the choice is yours to make, and the responsibility from that decision is yours as well."

◀   *Matthew 10:16*   ▶

Behold, I am sending you out as sheep in the midst of wolves, so be wise as serpents and innocent as doves.

Not everyone has the best in mind for us.

Jesus said it this way: We, who are His followers, are to be like sheep, but those we meet will be like wolves.

They will try to consume us with teeth, claws, and many vicious snarls.

We are to be as wise as serpents. The implication is that we are to be prudent in our dealings with those who try to bring us down. We must avoid conflict when we can.

We must also be as innocent as doves. We must maintain a simplicity in our dealings, show integrity, and respond with humility in tense situations.

Success is our choice. How we achieve it is up to us. When we choose the better path, we'll find success is especially sweet.

— Day 136 —

"Every excuse you make is one step backward from your goal."

◀ Matthew 7:7-8 ▶

Ask, and it will be given to you; seek, and you will find; knock, and it will be opened to you. For everyone who asks receives, and the one who seeks finds, and to the one who knocks it will be opened.

Try walking up the down escalator.

It's possible. With enough effort, you can make it to the top.

But wait! Pause just for a moment, and all your effort is undone. You're back where you started, at the bottom.

We must determine to keep moving forward. Our eyes must be on our goal.

We can make it to the top. Ask for strength, and we'll find it. Seek for courage, and it will be there. Knock on the door of opportunity, and we will be invited in.

God is our constant helper and moral support. He arranges our lives to benefit His will for us. When we trust in Him, our goal comes closer every day.

— Day 137 —

*"Take a look at your goal, what you desire,
and ask yourself what the price of success
is and if it is worth the cost, not only to
yourself, but to those around you, as well."*

◄| *Hebrews 10:24* |►

*And let us consider how to stir up one another to love
and good works.*

It's not just about us. It's about all of us.

That should be a repeated theme for anyone who is Christ-centered.

Our goal for success can't exclude those around us.

Our spouse, our coworkers, our children, our parents, and all those we spend time with daily. They pay the cost of our achievement, also.

Are we willing for them to give up the same things we're willing to sacrifice?

Do they think it's worth it?

When our triumph becomes everyone's, we'll truly move into a higher realm of success.

— Day 138 —

"Never underestimate the task at hand or the obstacles in your path. Success requires determination and attention."

2 Timothy 4:7   ►►

I have fought the good fight, I have finished the race, I have kept the faith.

Stick-to-itiveness.

That's a real word, but more importantly, it's a real concept.

We must stick to the task at hand if we're ever to complete it. If we get distracted, and our attention goes this way or that, we'll never reach our goal.

Is our goal to work from home? Set the phone to mute, and only check it every hour.

Are we going for a college degree? Forget the parties and crack open the textbooks.

Changing the diet for fitness' sake? Don't even walk by the chocolate shop.

It's our determination and our attention to our goal that helps us finish the race. Fight the good fight. Reach your goal.

— Day 139 —

"Don't fear what you may face, for you have the capability to overcome any obstacle in your path."

◀   Acts 17:11   ▶

Now these Jews were more noble than those in Thessalonica; they received the word with all eagerness, examining the Scriptures daily to see if these things were so.

Some people measure up better than others.

We don't like to think that, but it's true. What makes the difference? Their willingness to put out extra effort.

Our capability to overcome the obstacles we face isn't dependent on the obstructions we encounter. It comes from within, from our commitment to plowing through, from us saying, "Get out of my way! I've got a day of success coming on!"

Then we knock the obstacles to the side, and we march on past. We head into our success with a fist raised high, success-speak on our tongue, and our voice calling out victoriously.

We measure up better when we make the extra effort, do the thing that seems too hard for others, and determine success will be ours.

— Day 140 —

"Defend your beliefs, fight for your desires, but never stand still."

◀   *Joel 3:10*   ▶

Beat your plowshares into swords, and your pruning hooks into spears; let the weak say, "I am a warrior."

We can't afford to live our lives as wimps, not if we want to accomplish our goal and find success.

What do we believe? In kindness, women's rights, or that fighting animal cruelty is worth our time?

Do we believe that no child should go to school hungry, or that churches have the right to worship as they wish?

When our beliefs underpin that goal, we can't let them be eroded by naysayers. Shuck them off. Cast them aside. Fight for that goal, so that we can reach our highest plateau of success.

No one will fight for us as hard as we can.

If we're standing still, the world's not. We're being left behind, and our success is fading before our eyes.

Post your beliefs on your fridge. Share them. Do them.

— Day 141 —

"Holding a grudge is like picking up a hot
stone. It burns the hand that touches it."

◀   *Ephesians 4:26*   ▶

Be angry and do not sin; do not let the sun go down on your anger.

A grudge, by definition, is deep seated and ongoing.

There are four steps to resolving a grudge.

1. Communicate. Express how you feel to the person who's offended you. Focus on the problem, not your feelings.

2. Listen. Be active in hearing what the other person has to say. Try to understand how they think.

3. Consider. Look for solutions. Bring in a third party. Be open to ideas that benefit both.

4. Win-win. Agree on an option that gives each person a measure of success. Just giving in won't ultimately resolve the conflict.

A grudge is a distraction to pursuing your goal. You can't let the grudge become your focus. Let it go. Be the peacemaker. Take the first step.

— Day 142 —

"Always and continually seek to improve yourself."

◀| 2 Timothy 2:16 |▶

But avoid irreverent babble, for it will lead people into more and more ungodliness.

There are two sides to every person, the yin and the yang, the black and the white, the good and the evil.

We have desires that pull us both ways, and it's our choice which way we go.

Do we give in to what's convenient, and slide along the easy path? Or do we choose the harder way, and work to become better than we've been?

Our best and foremost way to effect a quick and apparent improvement in our life is to watch what we say. Zip our lips, when it comes to casual talk. Avoid gossip, and only say what's kind and uplifting.

We will be improved in the sight of others, and they will see us as better than we are. We will become better, also, as we move toward our goal.

— Day 143 —

"Remember to lead by example, as that is often the most influential manner to instigate change."

◀ *Philippians 3:17* ▶

Brothers, join in imitating me, and keep your eyes on those who walk according to the example you have in us.

We find pictures of kids adorable.

A boy with his dad, both shaving before a mirror, the boy's face lathered up with cream.

Or a daughter watching her mother getting ready to go out, wearing her mother's high heels, wanting to be just like her.

Children become what we show them, not what we say.

How much more so our coworkers, our church fellowship, and the people we interact with on the highway?

If we live aggressively, others will mimic our behavior and become like us. When we're kind, they mimic that, also.

To improve the world, let's improve us. We lead by example, and our finest example is found in the Bible. To be like Jesus is our goal.

— Day 144 —

*"There are those who would seek to derail
you from your path. Stay steadfast, and
you will not fail to reach your goal."*

◀ Isaiah 40:31 ▶

*But they who wait for the LORD shall renew their strength; they
shall mount up with wings like eagles; they shall run and not be
weary; they shall walk and not faint.*

In the Old West, train robbers had a simple way to get the
gold. They piled logs on the tracks, and either the train came to
a stop, or the engine hit the logs and was derailed.

The engine and many of its cars would fly off the rail and
become a target for the thieves to help themselves to whatever
they wanted.

A lookout was necessary to ensure the safety of the train, its
contents, and all its passengers.

The Bible is our lookout and our example for Christ-like
behavior. When our standards are God's standards, we will
mount up like eagles, and we won't be affected by the logs on the
tracks. We'll soar over them and find success, run and not grow
tired, walk and not feel exhaustion, and we will reach our goal.

— Day 145 —

"You must work diligently and with
perseverance to succeed."

◀   *Revelation 2:2*   ▶

I know your works, your toil and your patient endurance, and how
you cannot bear with those who are evil, but have tested those who
call themselves apostles and are not, and found them to be false.

The Panama Canal is one of the wonders of the modern world. The French began construction in 1881, only to give up in frustration within 20 years. The United States took over, and the first official transit was completed in 1914.

It had taken 33 years, but the canal was complete.

Some goals require more diligence than others. The French failed, but the United States wasn't daunted. They persevered with the determination that it could be done.

Your goal isn't out of your reach, not if you determine that it's attainable.

Don't think it might be. That's a goal already defeated. Determine it's possible, and envision yourself already there. What you can picture in your mind is what you'll achieve.

— Day 146 —

*"Do not fear the unknown; for from the
unknown some of your greatest gifts and
achievements will come."*

1 Peter 4:10

*As each has received a gift, use it to serve one another, as good
stewards of God's varied grace:*

The microwave oven was invented when a magnetron from a radar array melted a bar of chocolate.

The Slinky toy came from an experiment to stabilize sensitive instruments aboard Navy ships.

Play-Doh was a failed wall cleaner. All the company did was remove the cleaning agent, and it became a favorite child's toy.

Dr. Harry Coover created a substance that frustratingly stuck to everything. He considered it a failure. We call it Super Glue.

Our very worst attribute, when applied to our situation properly, can become our greatest asset.

Everything we have, who we are, and what we bring to the table are gifts from God. As good stewards, it's up to us to use what we're given to achieve the goal we set out to achieve.

— Day 147 —

*"To achieve great things, you must first
have faith that they are possible."*

◄ Romans 10:17 ►

*So faith comes from hearing, and hearing through the word of
Christ.*

Research. That's what reading the Bible is. We're learning the nature of God, how He interacts with humanity, and what we can expect from Him.

Through our study, we learn to trust in Him, building faith.

It works the same in our daily lives. When we set a goal, we read as much as possible about it. We learn the nature of our goal, how it impacts us and the world around us, and what we must do to achieve it.

Through our new knowledge, we learn to believe in our ability to achieve our goal. We learn faith.

It's through our faith that we believe we can achieve our goal.

When we are well-informed, that's when nothing can hold us back.

— Day 148 —

"No amount of plans will ever change your life without your actions to back them up!"

◀   *1 Samuel 26:25*   ▶

Then Saul said to David, "Blessed be you, my son David! You will do many things and will succeed in them." So David went his way, and Saul returned to his place.

Here's a challenge for the day:

Go into your closet and look at the soles of your shoes.

Forget the new ones. Check the shoes you wear daily. How worn are they?

Now look at your computer keyboard. Are the keys polished with constant use?

Our success comes in *doing many things.* That doesn't mean to be wishy-washy or flighty. We aren't to have numerous half-finished projects laying around. We're to get focused and *stay busy.*

What projects have you finished recently that are directly related to your goal? None, one, two? It's time to get on the ball.

— Day 149 —

"If something negatively influences your life, then change what is negatively influencing you. If you can't change it, get rid of it."

◀   *Ephesians 5:11*   ▶

Take no part in the unfruitful works of darkness, but instead expose them.

Old-fashioned strings of Christmas lights had an especially vexing characteristic. When one light went out, they all did.

The only option was to change out bulb after bulb until we discovered the faulty light. It was frustrating to go through the whole string, only to have to start over.

If more than one bulb had failed, it was better just to throw the whole string out and replace it with something improved.

Life will negatively influence us. It's the human condition. We must change that influence to a positive one. If we try, and the influence won't desist, toss it out. If it's a job, gone! A negative friend? Out the door! Too many credit cards? Chopped up! Junk food? In the garbage.

What keeps us from our goal isn't worth having around. What we can't keep is only fit for the garbage heap.

— Day 150 —

*"With faith in your success, you are
already on the correct path."*

◀ *Psalm* 16:11 ▶

*You make known to me the path of life; in your presence there is
fullness of joy; at your right hand are pleasures forevermore.*

Hiking mountain trails is a treat enjoyed by over 47 million
Americans every year.

About 2,000 of those get lost.

They start out, intending to reach the end, and they never
make it. They have faith they can find their way, and somehow,
they get off the correct path.

If they had a trail map, they might have found their way.

Our trail map to successfully reaching our goal is our diligent
preparation, our earnest study of the Bible, and our constant
application of our knowledge toward our desired end.

God shines His light on our footsteps, guiding us in our
walk. Our faith gives us the confidence we'll reach our goal. We'll
find our fullness of joy in Him when we complete the trail.

— Day 151 —

*"Those who act are the ones who will
make a positive difference in the world."*

◀ι   *1 Corinthians 10:31*   ι▶

*So, whether you eat or drink, or whatever you do, do all to the glory
of God.*

Our smallest actions make the biggest difference.

We can't say, "Oh, that's a little sin. It doesn't matter."

Those are the important ones. They're gateway behaviors. Little lies, justified by social necessities. Financial falsehoods, to save a few dollars.

A way out of trouble, if only we adjust the truth.

We are being watched, and not by the government. Friends, coworkers, our children. The little things we do are the ones they'll remember years down the road.

Smile when you mow the grass. Remember to greet the car wash attendant. Laugh at your son's joke and your daughter's comical dance.

Do it to as unto the Lord, and learn to live while you laugh.

— Day 152 —

"The most important thing you can do to achieve success is serve the LORD with your entire heart."

◄   *Colossians 3:16*   ▐►

Let the word of Christ dwell in you richly, teaching and admonishing one another in all wisdom, singing psalms and hymns and spiritual songs, with thankfulness in your hearts to God.

True service to God affects every part of our lives.

It's not just about Sunday morning service, a twenty in the plate, and filling in the front of the family Bible.

Our Christian experience benefits us in all manner of ways.

1. It teaches us using God-given wisdom accumulated over thousands of years.
2. We internalize a positive outlook based on the upbeat psalms and other passages from the Bible.
3. We learn thankfulness, a vital aspect of success in any endeavor.

Christianity isn't just for the weekend. When we apply it to our lives daily, it lifts our aspirations, brightens our outlook on life, and lets others see us as someone they want to have around.

— Day 153 —

*"Do not feel rushed, for it will only cause
you to make mistakes."*

◀ *Proverbs 27:23* ▶

*Know well the condition of your flocks, and give attention to your
herds.*

What does your bank account look like?

Do you know the exact balance of your investments?

Can you quote how much you spent to fuel your car last
month?

When we know the state of our finances, we're better able to
check off the boxes on the way to our goal.

It works with our families, too.

Who was at your daughter's sleepover? Which friend did
your son go to the game with?

What color of flowers does your spouse enjoy best?

We can't bypass the details on the way to the top. Taking
time to be informed will improve every decision we make.

— Day 154 —

"It is far better to do things correctly the first time, rather than repeat the process several times to get it correct."

◀| Psalm 119:105 |▶

Your word is a lamp to my feet and a light to my path.

Instruction manuals have a purpose.

We may not use them, but we should. We can bypass much of the trial-and-error that opens up opportunities for mistakes.

There's one other thing an instruction manual forces us to do, to pace ourselves one step at a time. The process is an ordered one, checking for the correct parts, using them in the correct sequence, and discovering the little details that could leave us undone later.

It's that little screw we leave out early in the process that will cause us to undo all our work and start over.

Our instruction manual for life is the Bible. We learn how to deal with other people, with our Lord, and with our plans for the future.

Success comes quicker when we follow the directions.

— Day 155 —

"Believing that success will be yours is only the first step. Before it can become a reality, you must also act on your belief."

James 2:24   ▶

You see that a person is justified by works and not by faith alone.

When we set our goal in life, we must believe it's possible, or it won't happen. We must have faith in ourselves.

There's more, though. It's like attending college. Just signing up for class isn't enough. We can believe we're getting a degree, but if we don't show up for the lectures, we won't receive a grade. We must participate to get credit.

In our spiritual walk, just believing in Christ isn't enough. It doesn't justify us before God. We must also live as Christ showed us. We must love others as ourselves and be compassionate to those in need.

Success comes in the same way. Take an online class. Put aside seed money. Contact people who are in the field you want to join. Volunteer. Get involved. Do something.

An athlete never won a game on the sideline. A successful businessman doesn't grow his business on the sofa. Act now!

— Day 156 —

"The potential for success is within you.
It's time to make the choice."

◀ Micah 6:8 ▶

He has told you, O man, what is good; and what does
the LORD require of you but to do justice, and to love kindness, and
to walk humbly with your God?

We can have the success we desire. The Bible gives us three basic steps to achieve our potential.

1. *We must do justice.* This is morality in its essence. If someone works for us, reward him or her. If we borrow money, pay the bill.
2. *We must love kindness.* Be polite. Help someone carry a heavy package. Offer to buy lunch.
3. *We must be humble before God.* We are to be conscious of His will in every moment of our day and how it affects our connections with others.

Master these three things, and we can't help but move ahead into success. We'll be tugged forward, inexorably drawn into what we want to become.

We'll find reaching our goal is as easy as 1, 2, 3.

— Day 157 —

"All it usually takes is to show people that there's a path available, and that path will lead to an improvement of their lives."

Psalm 119:18   ▶

Open my eyes, that I may behold wondrous things out of your law.

We know what we're familiar with.

That seems obvious, but how many times have we said, "Duh! They just don't get it!"

Maybe they haven't been shown what they need to know.

- Teach someone to use a checkbook.
- Explain their smart phone.
- Help them change the oil in their lawnmower.
- Share a stock tip and how to trade online.
- Recommend a college course.
- Mentor someone to open the possibilities in his or her life.

Our success needs to be shared. People who want it will learn from us, and their lives will be improved by our actions.

— Day 158 —

"There are always risks on your path to achieve your goals."

◀   *Hebrews 12:3*   ▶

Consider him who endured from sinners such hostility against himself, so that you may not grow weary or fainthearted.

How big is your goal?

Would someone kill you to prevent you from achieving it?

What!?! Kill me over the goal I set? It's happened.

Jesus had a goal, to provide redemption for all mankind. He was crucified on the cross to keep His goal from becoming reality.

Jesus faced His risks head on, and He didn't shy away.

Every goal-oriented path carries risks. They might be financial, emotional, or physical. We invest in our new company, take a chance on marriage, or aim for the peak of Mount Everest. We run a risk in each of these. We can't let that curb our enthusiasm. We simply prepare a little harder.

Jesus risked everything for His success. We must step out in the confidence that we are able to reach our goal.

— Day 159 —

"You have a choice. You can either make excuses for yourself and your actions, or you can achieve success. You can't do both."

◀ *Genesis 3:13* ▶

Then the LORD God said to the woman, "What is this that you have done?" The woman said, "The serpent deceived me, and I ate."

Patterns of ingrained behavior dictate how we live our lives.

If we continually get up mid-morning, we'll never achieve a job on an early morning talk show. It would be a bad fit.

To blame it on the time of day is an excuse, not a reason.

We must break our old habits if we want to alter the path we're on. Forget the late, late movie. Take to setting our alarm. Shower the night before and lay out our clothes before bedtime.

If we are focused on our future, making a change in our present is no big deal. It's quite easy, because we know that what we're giving up will bring us great rewards.

What do you want? What's in the way? Toss it; change it; throw all the old habits out the door. It's time for our success!

— Day 160 —

"You can't be afraid of hard work if you desire success."

◀   *Proverbs 18:9*   ▶

Whoever is slack in his work is a brother to him who destroys.

What's the harm in taking a few minutes of our employer's time for personal business?

It's just a phone call, or a quick purchase on the Internet.

It can't hurt our efficiency that much.

It's hard work that creates success. Lazing off is the same as taking a sledge hammer and bashing our employer's business.

How? Every moment not on task robs the employer of the funds that go in to our paycheck. We've stolen productivity, product image, and company resources.

We are a resource. If we work hard, our company prospers. They can't do it alone. We can't do it without them.

When we own the business, this principle is even more vital. We can never lose focus, if we're to stay successful. We're the example everyone else is following.

— Day 161 —

"It may feel as if all your options have closed before you, but you are only lost if you stop walking forward."

◄I   Proverbs 14:15   I►

The simple believes everything, but the prudent gives thought to his steps.

The short-sighted can't see past the problems of today.

A home remodeler must be able to envision what a ruined house can become before he tears down the first wall.

A stock broker knows that falling prices provide the best opportunity to pick up good deals.

A store owner sees the end-of-season sales as a chance to restock with fresh merchandise.

If the door to your opportunity seems to close, what other doors are there? What windows can you climb through? Is there a hatchet you can use to hack through the ceiling?

Using Success-Speak, today's problems become just that: *today's* problems. Not tomorrow's problems. They are a leaping off point to something new and better, a fresh chance for success.

— Day 162 —

"Don't fear losing what you never had in the first place."

◀   Psalm 106:1   ▶

Praise the LORD! Oh give thanks to the LORD, for he is good, for his steadfast love endures forever!

A poor man owned a bare, windswept mountain slope. He hoped to harvest trees from it one day and provide for his family. He borrowed all he could to plant seedlings on the slopes.

His wife grew ill, and he was offered a price for his mountain that would pay the doctor's bill and give him enough to live modestly for the rest of his life. He remembered his dream of harvesting trees, and he was afraid to give up what he'd started. Instead, he worked extra hours at menial jobs to pay his bills, wearing out his body and becoming frail.

He died before the first trees could be harvested.

If we're so worried about what we'll miss out on that we forget to enjoy today, is our potential success worth it?

There's more to success than a corner office and a fancy car. It's in how we live our lives, and the journey we've taken.

— Day 163 —

*"Forgiveness is the only choice if you want
to move forward in your life."*

◁   *Ephesians 4:32*   ▷

*Be kind to one another, tenderhearted, forgiving one another, as
God in Christ forgave you.*

Refusing to forgive makes people sick.

Yep, sick, sick, sick.

We're talking cardiovascular issues and high blood pressure. Brain hemorrhages. It can cause us to become anorexic or bulimic.

It can even precipitate serious depression, which can lead to a deep, dark place.

When we forgive, our stress levels drop, leading to an improved mental outlook, and our overall health skyrockets.

Forgiveness is the bedrock of a civil and healthy society.

It's the foundation of a successful business.

It's absolutely necessary if we're to reach our goal.

— Day 164 —

"You have a choice. You can either cower in the corner or overcome those who would seek to destroy you."

◂   *Matthew 18:15*   ▸

If your brother sins against you, go and tell him his fault, between you and him alone. If he listens to you, you have gained your brother.

We're to be peacemakers.

That works well in most cases, but don't misread the scriptures. We aren't to be wimps.

We want to reconcile with our brother, if possible, but if we can't, and our brother is determined to undermine our journey toward our goal, we're to shake the dust of his house off our shoes and move on.

Today's verse says *if he listens*. If he doesn't, our responsibility is done. It's time to refocus and aim for our future.

We're never, never to cower in fear because someone comes against us. God hasn't given us a spirit of fear, but of a sound mind (2 Timothy 1:7). A sound mind is one that moves out of the way of destruction and into the light.

— Day 165 —

*"If you never stop learning and growing,
then you will continually be achieving
greater levels of success."*

◀◁   *Proverbs 1:5*   ▷▶

*Let the wise hear and increase in learning, and the one who
understands obtain guidance.*

Who's the better basketball player, Michael Jordan at 6'6" or Muggsy Bogues at 5'5"?

The judgment call is yours, but when a player keeps growing, that's an advantage in this sport.

What about in achieving the goal we've set for ourselves? Is there ever a time it's okay to stop growing?

Doctors, nurses, and dentists need to update their knowledge and skills to provide us the best care.

Lawyers and paralegals, also, get to head back to school.

Architects, supervisors, and project managers, all!

We grow when we learn, and when we learn, we're moving forward. The more we move forward, the greater our success will be. Learn and grow, and you'll reach your goal.

— Day 166 —

*"Dwelling in the past will not allow you to
make progress toward the future."*

◀ᴵ *Luke 11:28* ᴵ▶

*But [Jesus] said, "Blessed rather are those who hear the word of
God and keep it!"*

Our lives are like being on a cruise ship, visiting one island each day.

Once we sail away, we can never revisit that island. What we've done there, the people we met, and the things we experienced are left behind.

We can remember them, but we can't return.

Living in the past is like jumping from our ship to swim back to an island we remember but can never find.

It's gone, lost forever, and if we continue to swim, the ocean will swallow us forever.

Jesus said, *Blessed rather . . .*

Rather than what? We are blessed when we move forward in life, in hearing the Bible, and in pursuing our goal.

— Day 167 —

"Knowledge is a bringer of success."

◀   *Proverbs 8:10*   ▶

Take my instruction instead of silver, and knowledge rather than choice gold.

Give a man a fish, and he'll eat for a day.

Teach him to fish, and he'll eat for a lifetime.

Everyone enjoys something for free. That's what birthdays are all about. Presents. Gifts. Something for nothing. More, more, more!

Yet what we work for has a deeper meaning.

Think of the first car you owned, that you paid for yourself. It made it special. Better. Worth your time to wax and polish the paint, whether it was old or new.

We learn by studying and by doing. What we learn makes us wise. Wisdom brings success.

When we offer prayers to God, let's ask for perseverance, endurance, and wisdom. If we have those, we'll eat for a lifetime.

— Day 168 —

*"Don't let one failure get you down . . . or
the next hundred."*

2 Corinthians 5:17   ▶

*Therefore, if anyone is in Christ, he is a new creation. The old has
passed away; behold, the new has come.*

Alexander Graham Bell is an icon in the world of communication.

He invented the telephone!

Yet what we don't know is that days after he filed his patent for the iconic device, he was hit was over 600 lawsuits. Did he give up? Of course not. He went on to invent a metal detector, a speedboat that set a word's record, and a wireless telephone – patented in 1880!

If Bell had been inclined to give up, our world would be very different today. If we give up, the world of tomorrow will be less than it could be. If we trip up, don't lay there; we can always stand again.

There's no rule that says we must stay down. The decision to move forward is ours alone. Let's brush off our knees and go!

— Day 169 —

"Success does not come easily. It requires hard work, patience, and the will to persist in your effort to succeed."

Proverbs 13:4   ▶

The soul of the sluggard craves and gets nothing, while the soul of the diligent is richly supplied.

The ant and the grasshopper.

It's a familiar fable designed to teach us that all play and no work means we might starve during challenging times.

If we're lazy, we don't eat. It's the hard workers who deserve a good meal.

When was the last time your back hurt? Or your calves?

If you work with your brain, it can hurt, too, literally. Hours of intense concentration can drain your energy reserves. The brain is 2 percent of your body weight but uses up to 20 percent of your calorie needs.

Nothing comes for free, not food and not success.

Let's be the diligent ant. We'll make it to our goal when we put our persistence to the test and overcome the rest.

— Day 170 —

"Success rarely falls into your lap; you must make the conscious decision to succeed before it can be yours."

2 Corinthians 12:12   ▶

The signs of a true apostle were performed among you with utmost patience, with signs and wonders and mighty works.

What's inside us tells the truth of who we are.

It's our true self.

Are we really focused on reaching our goal? What are some signs we should look for?

Paul says the proof he's a man of God are his patience, and the signs, wonders, and mighty deeds he did.

What are our signs of success?

Have we taken the time to prepare? Do we exhibit the successful behaviors we're trying to emulate? Are people amazed that we've come so far? Are we doing everything we know to move toward our success?

Success doesn't find us on our sofa. It walks the street with us, and it leads us forward toward our goal.

— Day 171 —

*"Those you associate with will leave a
lasting impression on you."*

◀   Acts 15:4   ▶

*When they came to Jerusalem, they were welcomed by the church
and the apostles and the elders, and they declared all that God had
done with them.*

Who do we want to be?

We have a choice, and it's not what you might think.

Look at each of your friends. Ask yourself if that's who you
would trade places with, if you could be anyone else in the world.

If you're spending time with that person, you're becoming
like him or her.

That's right. You're taking on his or her characteristics.

Let's choose people who'll help us toward our goal. Our
friends should be goal-focused, learning-oriented, and willing to
forgo instant gratification to meet long-term goals.

Who do we want to be? The question's still there. The choice
is ours, and it's reflected in the friends at our side.

— Day 172 —

"Each day you move forward, you are progressing toward true success."

◀︎   *Psalm 90:12*   ▶︎

So teach us to number our days that we may get a heart of wisdom.

Our days are like a jar of leaves.

Each day we take one out, and by evening, its color is gone, and we can crumple it in our hands.

The jar is still full, but we have no way to know how many are still inside.

We can only use the wisdom we have to enjoy one day at a time. It's vital that we don't waste any of our leaves. One day we'll open our jar, and it will be our last one.

Our day to move forward is now. To waste a leaf by doing nothing is toss it aside while it's still soft and green.

We never even get to see it turn red and gold in the autumn of its life.

The beauty of life is in living today, right now, this very minute. The beauty of success is striving for our goal every day.

— Day 173 —

*"Just because somebody understands
what they need to do doesn't mean that
they know how to do it."*

◀ 1 Corinthians 13:12 ▶

*For now we see in a mirror dimly, but then face to face. Now I
know in part; then I shall know fully, even as I have been fully
known.*

1 Corinthians 13:12 is one of the most poetic scriptures in
the Bible.

What does it mean? *Now we see in a mirror dimly . . .*

There are some things we simply can't understand. It doesn't
mean we're dumb, just that we haven't received that information.

Paul goes on to say, *then I shall know fully . . .*

All around us are people stumbling, wishing for success, and
only finding failure. They are searching in a mirror just like Paul.

We may not know the answer to what's on the other side of
Paul's mirror, but we can help others by offering them guidance,
both spiritual and toward their goals.

Our knowledge shared becomes a vast storehouse of good.

— Day 174 —

"You can be part of those who will change the world, but you must be willing to do what you know is right."

Galatians 5:22-23   ▶

But the fruit of the Spirit is love, joy, peace, patience, kindness, goodness, faithfulness, gentleness, self-control; against such things there is no law.

Marin Luther King, Jr. fought a war against inequality with words of love.

Mahatma Gandhi championed change in a peaceful manner.

Mother Teresa cared for the sick and the poor and received the Nobel Peace Prize.

These people changed the world using love, joy, peace, patience, kindness, goodness, faithfulness, gentleness, and self-control.

We change the world in the same way, using the same skills. We find our strength in God, who is our champion and defender.

Our goal is within our reach. When we move forward by doing what's right, we make our goal worth the effort.

— Day 175 —

"Do not regret your mistakes. Understand how you made the mistake, find a solution to prevent it from occurring again, and take heart in the knowledge that you have improved."

◀   1 Peter 5:7   ▶

Casting all your anxieties on him, because he cares for you.

Regret is a fiery coal.

Whoever picks it up is quickly burned.

We can't go backwards. Our mistake is already done. It must become a learning experience to vault us forward into something new.

We need to toss our solution onto our regret, extinguishing the flame and moving forward.

God can help us move ahead. Our plan for improvement can ease our remorse. Our new situation will rebuild our confidence. Our continued forward motion will convince the world we're sincere.

We need to wear the blinders of success. What's to the side can't be allowed to distract us. What's behind is of no importance. Only tomorrow is in our vision, and it will be ours.

— Day 176 —

"Having patience will allow you to complete your tasks far more efficiently."

◀ *Ephesians 6:4* ▶

Fathers, do not provoke your children to anger, but bring them up in the discipline and instruction of the Lord.

Conflicts create hard feelings.

In the workplace, kind words go far.

When working at a task, taking our time minimizes mistakes.

You can't add the eggs after the cake comes out of the oven.

It's all about patience and being careful with what we do. If we yell at our children, we stir up hard feelings that can last for decades. If an architect makes a mistake in the plans, the whole project may fail. Planning for our goal is a long-term endeavor, and we must allow the time it takes.

If we rush our timeline to success, we're apt to be forced to start again. Success-Speak can keep us on track along the way.

If it's worth doing, it's worth doing right the first time, in our jobs, in our homes, and in our efforts to reach our goal.

— Day 177 —

"Take responsibility for your actions."

◀   *Romans 13:7*   ▶

*Pay to all what is owed to them: taxes to whom taxes are owed,
revenue to whom revenue is owed, respect to whom respect is owed,
honor to whom honor is owed.*

A contract is a promise to pay.

When we have an estimate on our house for work to be done,
and we sign on the dotted line, we do more than write our name.
We enter into an agreement that's binding in a court of law.

It becomes a legal matter.

We have a moral and contractual obligation to do what we've
agreed. Our actions have consequences, and living up to them
reveals the strength of our commitment to our success.

When we're heading up the ladder toward our goal, we need
to be careful not to step on the fingers of those below us. They
are our resource for continued forward motion.

Success is teamwork. When we reach the top, we're all there.

— Day 178 —

"Do not strive for success blindly. You must have goals, a point you are aiming to reach."

◀   *Psalm 37:5*   ▶

Commit your way to the LORD; trust in him, and he will act.

Watch a child chase a piñata.

He's blindfolded. He's spun around. He has no idea where to go. His chance of hitting the paper toy is slim.

When our goals change daily, or we say we want to succeed, and yet we never prepare, we've put on a blindfold, we've let our choices spin us around and make us dizzy, and we're swinging like crazy, not knowing if we'll connect or not.

Imagine a college hopeful, and when she goes in, she never attends the same class. Her chances of graduating get slimmer with each visit.

Have we written our goal? Is it posted on our fridge? Is it on our social media feed? Do we talk about it to everyone we see?

When our success is important to us, everyone will know.

— Day 179 —

"Some people just need to be pointed in the correct direction."

◀ Proverbs 3:27 ▶

Do not withhold good from those to whom it is due, when it is in your power to do it.

Lead by example.

Think of the people who've made a difference in our lives.

A grandparent, a coach, or a neighbor. How did they set an example for us? How did they point us in the correct direction?

Did they support us at a critical time, either with advice or money? Maybe they were there when no one else was.

Who can we point in the right direction?

Our granddaughter? The pastor of our church? A college student struggling with an innovative business idea?

Get out there. Do it. Offer advice. Provide money, if that's what they need. Shift their track. Guide them the right direction.

Each of us can better other people's lives. Now is the time.

— Day 180 —

"Ask yourself if the risk to achieve your goal is worth the potential consequences. If not, take a step back, assess the situation, and find an alternate path to your success."

◀   *Matthew 5:1*   ▶

Seeing the crowds, [Jesus] went up on the mountain, and when he sat down, his disciples came to him.

Plans sometimes fall apart.

Even Jesus had to make alternate arrangements from time to time. Matthew 5:1 tells us that upon *seeing the crowds, He went up on the mountain.* That wasn't Jesus' original plan. He wanted to avoid the crowd. Yet, the following verse begins one of the best-loved passages in the New Testament, the Beatitudes.

All from a change in plans.

When we step back to reevaluate, that's an opportunity for something better to happen. Our alternative path to our success can lead us to something bigger and brighter than we ever expected.

What's your goal? Is it in sight? Never be afraid to rethink the path you're taking, research your options, and see if there's a better way.

— Day 181 —

"Never underestimate your goal."

Exodus 20:11   ▶

*For in six days the LORD made heaven and earth, the sea, and all
that is in them, and rested on the seventh day. Therefore
the LORD blessed the Sabbath day and made it holy.*

We can learn two things from this passage in Exodus.

1. God had a big job to do. The biggest. He had all creation to form and He chose to do it in just six days.
2. Once He was through, He sat back and rested for a day.

Reaching our goal takes a tremendous amount of effort. We
should never minimize what we put into it or the effort required
to achieve it.

It's good for us to take out time to rest. Go to the beach.
Spend a weekend in the mountains. Ride that bike. Go to the car
show. Enjoy an evening with friends. Take the time to connect
with people.

It's what God did, after all. He completed His goals and
rested for a whole day.

— Day 182 —

"To deny Jesus is to reject your future prosperity."

Proverbs 15:15   ▶

All the days of the afflicted are evil, but the cheerful of heart has a continual feast.

Following Jesus is a direct path to our planned success. The Bible sets up our parameters for reaching our goal.

1. Work hard every day (Proverbs 13:11)
2. Budget your income (Luke 14:28)
3. Pay down your debt (Proverbs 22:7)
4. Fund your savings generously (1 Corinthians 16:2)
5. Don't overextend yourself (Ecclesiastes 5:5)
6. Pay the taxes you owe (Mark 12:17)
7. Make wise investments (Matthew 25:20)
8. Research your investments (Proverbs 14:15)
9. Give to charities (Proverbs 28:27)
10. Work at your job efficiently (Ecclesiastes 10:10)
11. Don't co-sign loans (Proverbs 17:18)
12. Use a financial advisor (Proverbs 15:22)
13. Save for retirement (Proverbs 13:22)

— Day 183 —

"Before you can reach for the future, you must first let go of what you are holding onto in the past."

◀ Revelation 21:4 ▶

He will wipe away every tear from their eyes, and death shall be no more, neither shall there be mourning, nor crying, nor pain anymore, for the former things have passed away.

A boat anchor has one purpose: to keep the boat from going anywhere.

The downside is that the boat *can't* go anywhere. It's stuck in one place and is no use to anyone.

Our boat anchors are bad relationships, pain we've suffered, and financial commitments from which we can't break free.

Those old things have passed away. We are reborn through Christ's spirit.

We must quit slogging through the mud of yesterday's tears. Our future is ahead of us. The past is on the other side of the sunset, and it's not filled with diamonds and fairy-tale dreams.

We must discard our useless anchors to reach our goal.

— Day 184 —

"Success is largely dependent on the effort put toward achieving it."

◀ Psalm 90:17 ▶

Let the favor of the Lord our God be upon us, and establish the work of our hands upon us; yes, establish the work of our hands!

The old axiom is: Work In = Work Out.

That's easy to understand. If we don't *put something in,* we won't *get something out.*

Say it another away: Don't show up for work and you won't get a paycheck.

When we give our best effort, God is faithful to bless our outcome. We'll find what we do goes twice as far when God's in it.

Do we really want success? A lot? That's our motivation. We do whatever it takes, a part-time job, babysitters, extra practice on the piano, ride-sharing to split the cost. We don't see the sacrifice; we see the goal growing closer and closer.

We know the work we put in is exactly what we'll get out.

— Day 185 —

"Just because there is a path doesn't mean you should walk it."

◀ *James 1:14* ▶

But each person is tempted when he is lured and enticed by his own desire.

Everything that glitters looks like gold.

That pretty girl. That handsome boy.

Or maybe it's the car we can't afford. We need to find a shortcut to our financial success, because we want it now.

To reach our goal takes patience. To reach it well takes research. To reach it quickly by bending the rules is a disaster.

Feldspar is a mineral that shines like gold. Miners years ago had to be wary. Land agents would sell claims based on deposits of feldspar, duping the miners into a false sense of success.

They were mining a useless product.

True gold can withstand the fire. Flame weeds out feldspar from gold. If it looks like gold, test it with the fire of patience and necessity. Only what passes the test helps us toward our goal.

— Day 186 —

*"Every day learn at least one new word,
and before long you will find that your
vocabulary is significantly more
impressive."*

◀   *Colossians 4:6*   ▶

*Let your speech always be gracious, seasoned with salt, so that you
may know how you ought to answer each person.*

Language is how we communicate.

The more words we know, the more specific we can be.

It's all about nuance. Touch . . . or caress. Laugh . . . or snicker. Ask . . . or plead. How we say it goes a long way in how our words are perceived.

If we want to be gracious, we must be able to interact with each person correctly. To better our chances at successfully reaching our goal, we need to continually improve our vocabulary, especially in the field we prefer.

Sports? Learn ace, bump-and-run, and hat trick. Finance? Bottom-up investing, codicil, and discretionary trust.

Let's learn the talk, so we can walk the walk straight into our success. When we speak like the pros, we'll soon reach our goal.

— Day 187 —

"If you see somebody in need, don't be afraid to stand up and help them. You might need their help someday."

◀ Psalm 72:12 ▶

For he delivers the needy when he calls, the poor and him who has no helper.

What about the homeless, perhaps the panhandler who stands at the stoplight?

Does he or she deserve our help?

Maybe a coworker who's having car trouble, or a neighbor who can't seem to mow the grass. Is that where we step in?

Maybe we volunteer at the downtown mission to feed the hungry on Thursday nights. Yes, that's it for us.

Whatever we choose, let's do something. Anything. If someone is in need, and we have the opportunity, it's our chance to put our focus on success into practice.

True success isn't just about our pocketbook becoming fat with riches. It's about how we share our riches with people who need our help. We must begin today.

— Day 188 —

"Seek to understand all that is around you so that you may succeed beyond what you thought possible."

◀   Proverbs 20:5   ▶

The purpose in a man's heart is like deep water, but a man of understanding will draw it out.

What we understand is what we're good at.

Did you successfully sell fruit as a teenager, going door-to-door? Providing personalized shopping might be your strong suit.

How about real estate? Maybe you remodeled your first house and sold it for a hefty profit. You've found a skill you're good at.

It helps when we team up with others. Our partner, however, must be loyal and knowledgeable in our field, or we risk being knocked off our path to success.

We must research our allies just as we research our goals. We should seek to understand everything around us, including each other, to not waste our focus on unnecessary distractions.

When we understand our goal, we're already halfway there.

— Day 189 —

"Success is usually achieved through many repeated efforts."

◀ Lamentations 3:21-23 ▶

But this I call to mind, and therefore I have hope: The steadfast love of the LORD never ceases; his mercies never come to an end; they are new every morning; great is your faithfulness.

A child's skinned knee is never fun.

As parents know, it's rarely the only one. Children fall, and it's our job to offer them consolation, perhaps a bandage, and the encouragement to get back up and try again.

God does the same for us, offering us hope when we fall and skin our proverbial knees. He's there in our failed marriages, bankrupt businesses, and our neighborhood conflicts gone awry.

He reassures us we're loved, helps us patch things up, and encourages us to get back on our path to success.

It likely won't be the only time, either. Our success will come to us eventually, no matter how many times we skin our knees.

We get there because we get back up and try again.

— Day 190 —

"Stay on your path, and under no circumstances let it be compromised by fallacies, doubts, or outward influences."

◀ Proverbs 25:28 ▶

A man without self-control is like a city broken into and left without walls.

Our boundaries define who we are.

They tell others what we will and won't tolerate, whether we can be pushed around, and if we're determined to achieve our goal.

Once we let our boundaries be breached, we've compromised our integrity, and our journey forward is in peril.

Study what people say to determine if it's fact or opinion. Take it with a grain of salt, until you can prove it.

Be polite but firm in stating your goal. Don't waver. It's your life, not someone else's.

Your motivation must come from within. Any other sort will fizzle out.

Our self-control dictates our future. Let's use it for success.

— Day 191 —

"Move forward wisely. Others will be affected by your actions, too."

John 14:31   ▶

But I do as the Father has commanded me, so that the world may know that I love the Father. Rise, let us go from here.

Jesus didn't want to die on the cross.

It's the story of the Garden of Gethsemane, when He prayed for the cup of His crucifixion to pass from Him.

Even so, Jesus knew what was at stake. The entire world would be affected—for the better—by His death at the hands of the Roman soldiers.

He died as His Father wished, to bring us salvation today.

How do our decisions affect those around us? As parents, neighbors, and coworkers? Are their lives made better by the choices we make?

Moving forward toward our goal is vital. Moving forward while mindful of those around us reveals the excellence we have inside.

— Day 192 —

"There is no problem that doesn't have a solution. It is up to you to find that solution."

◂ Proverbs 3:5-6 ▸

Trust in the LORD with all your heart, and do not lean on your own understanding. In all your ways acknowledge him, and he will make straight your paths.

Math is an amazing field.

For the math enthusiasts among us, we look forward to the challenges we work out. For others, it's a mystery how it works.

Here's the thing about math. It works, even when we don't understand it. Apply the rules, and everything falls into place.

If we try to figure out life for ourselves, we'll fall flat every time. The problems we face will overwhelm us.

Hand them to God. Trust in Him. We don't have to understand how He works. We apply His love, and everything falls into place.

One God, plus one of us, equals the most important goal already reached!

— Day 193 —

"You have three very simple choices in life. Move backward, stand still, or move forward. The time to make that choice is now."

◀ *John 5:8* ▶

Jesus said to him, "Get up, take up your bed, and walk."

Draw a timeline.

You remember, like in social studies. Mark each end with a dot and label one as Today and the other as My Goal.

Now fill in all the things reaching your goal will require.

As you complete them, mark them off. Use ink so they can't be erased.

You never want to go backwards.

If the crippled man had said to Jesus, "Oh, not today," he would have remained there until he died. To receive Jesus' healing, he had to move forward. He had to get up and *walk*.

Your journey toward your goal requires the same commitment. You are to get up and *walk*. You must head toward your goal and keep moving. Your opportunity to move into your success is today.

— Day 194 —

"Your knowledge is only limited by how much you're willing to learn."

◀| Psalm 25:4-5 |▶

Make me to know your ways, O LORD; teach me your paths. Lead me in your truth and teach me, for you are the God of my salvation; for you I wait all the day long.

How smart can we become?

Do we quit learning when we leave school?

Is a post-graduate degree the only way to prove we have a brain?

Just waking up in the morning floods us with knowledge. Whether we choose to retain it is another matter.

Ask a construction worker about his tools, or a gardener about the best place to plant roses. She'll be able to tell us when to plant and where, and even how often we need to water.

It's about paying attention to life. It's in our attitude, not in our seat time in a classroom.

If we pay attention to God, He will teach us, too.

— Day 195 —

"The ability to move past your failures is critical for success."

◀ *Proverbs 24:16* ▶

For the righteous falls seven times and rises again, but the wicked stumble in times of calamity.

Donald Trump was elected president in the fall of 2016, taking office the next January.

He presided in the highest office in the land. It was quite an achievement.

It's more impressive when we learn he declared bankruptcy six times between 1992 and 2009, according to *The Washington Post.*

Whatever your opinion of the man, the fact remains that he stumbled badly six times, got back up, and earned the electoral votes of the nation.

He didn't let his mistakes keep him from moving toward his goal.

The decision is ours. Make it now. Get back up. Be a success.

— Day 196 —

"If you do not like the way your life is going, then you must be the one to take a stand and change it."

◀   Matthew 16:18   ▶

And I tell you, you are Peter, and on this rock I will build my church, and the gates of hell shall not prevail against it.

Peter was one of the least promising of Jesus' disciples.

- He needed Jesus' parables explained on 3 occasions.
- He tried to prevent the children from coming to Jesus.
- He was rebuked by Jesus who described him as "Satan," and he repeatedly took offense at the other disciples.
- He refused to let Jesus wash his feet.
- He fell asleep at Gethsemane.
- He publicly denied Jesus *more than once.*

And yet, Peter turned his life around and became the founding rock upon which Christ's church is built.

If you don't like your life, it's never too late to change it. Make a goal, start a plan, and stick to it.

— Day 197 —

"There's a fine line between just wanting more and that of greed."

◀   1 Timothy 6:9   ▶

But those who desire to be rich fall into temptation, into a snare, into many senseless and harmful desires that plunge people into ruin and destruction.

Wanting to live well isn't an issue.

Much of our motivation for success in life comes from the milestones we click off along the way.

It's our bucket list, the things we've dreamed of and finally get to do. Paris. A sports car. An extra bathroom just for guests. A swimming pool or a vacation home.

There's nothing wrong with these, if they don't consume our concern for our fellow man. When *people* no longer come before *possessions,* we've got a problem.

We call it greed. Success-Speak points us a better direction.

We must have a goal. We must also remember to include in that goal the people we live with. We travel forward as a team.

— Day 198 —

"If you only make excuses, then making excuses will be the only thing you're good at."

◀   *Proverbs 26:13*   ▶

The sluggard says, "There is a lion in the road! There is a lion in the streets!"

What's your excuse for not moving toward your goal?

A lion in the street? *A lion in the street!?!* Someone must be kidding. That's no more than an excuse for being lazy.

How about these:

"My family doesn't attend college."

"We're not business people."

"I can't get up early."

"My car is undependable."

If you want to make excuses, you can do that all day long. It's time to make a difference. It's your moment to move forward toward your goal. Get up. Break out. Step forward. Determine that this is your day for everything to change.

— Day 199 —

"Without a goal and an objective, you will be without direction."

◀   *Revelation 3:16*   ▶

So, because you are lukewarm, and neither hot nor cold, I will spit you out of my mouth.

Tea or coffee at room temperature tastes nasty.

If it's not hot or cold, the flavor becomes unappealing, and we want to toss it out.

It's being one or the other that brings out the alluring qualities of the beverages. Hot coffee or cold, we choose. Both are excellent. Tea is the same. Hot or cold, the preference is ours.

When we have direction in our lives, when we stick to our guns and keep our focus, we earn people's respect. We're either hot or cold, going this way or that, committed to a purpose.

It's the wishy-washy, directionless person that we want to wash down the drain.

Get a folder. Write your top goal inside. Track your progress. Pull it out and read it every day. Move toward success.

— Day 200 —

"Does failure at an attempt to succeed mean you have lost? No. It only shows that you have found one way not to succeed."

◀   Deuteronomy 8:18   ▶

You shall remember the LORD your God, for it is he who gives you power to get wealth, that he may confirm his covenant that he swore to your fathers, as it is this day.

Success isn't a straight, uphill shot.

Sometimes we must circle the mountain to find a clear path to the top.

A wrong turn isn't a failure. We have the power to reach our goal. Our success is within our grasp. Our misstep tells us one way not to get there, and we take a different route.

We try again.

God is our covenant-maker. He enables us to be successful. He provides us the power to get wealth. He charges us with fresh ideas and the drive to move forward.

Never write down your failures. Only list your successes. They will motivate you to keep surging toward your goal.

— Day 201 —

"There is always an alternative, whether it is obvious or not."

◀   Luke 3:14   ▶

Soldiers also asked him, "And we, what shall we do?" And he said to them, "Do not extort money from anyone by threats or by false accusation, and be content with your wages."

Some professions seem obvious.

A football player is meant to smash into someone else.

A sanitation worker clears away what the rest of us leave behind.

A doctor heals those who are sick.

A teacher imparts knowledge to the less wise.

The soldiers in Jesus' day were the authority with near-unlimited power. They ruled by fear and intimidation.

Jesus gave them a different way. Be honest. Be kind. Be content with what you have. Whatever our occupation demands from us in our journey toward success, taking the high road makes our achievements worthwhile.

— Day 202 —

"You should always plan for the worst but hope for the best."

◀ *Romans 12:12* ▶

Rejoice in hope, be patient in tribulation, be constant in prayer.

It's the unexpected flood that washes away our home. If we knew it was coming, we wouldn't have built there.

How can we mitigate the loss? Insurance, of course. We spread the risk among many people, and no one is hit with too high a bill.

We must keep our premiums paid, naturally. We're planning for the worst, although we hope it never happens.

We want our plans to go off without a hitch. Yet, experience tells us differently. Bad things happen when we least expect them: the car's engine bites the dust; a pipe in the basement bursts; the dog needs emergency care; or a dozen other roadblocks.

Our solution is to 1. Rejoice, 2. Be patient, 3. Be constant in our appeals to God.

Our success will be ours, if we're well prepared.

— Day 203 —

"Stand tall, know what your reasons are, and never let anybody pull you from your path."

◀ Proverbs 16:3 ▶

Commit your work to the LORD, and your plans will be established.

Herding dogs include many breeds, from Shepherds to Corgis.

The most intelligent is the Border Collie. This magnificent animal does its job by running, barking, making strong eye contact, and nipping at the livestock's heels, if necessary.

The Collie knows its job, and it lets nothing prevent it from doing its duty. It's committed to its charges, and it refuses to let them go astray.

When our path is well defined, and we're committed to moving forward, we'll find our success. We may have to run around a bit, get in people's faces, and even nip at their heels, but they'll know we're serious about moving ahead.

Our determination is what people see. They'll move to the side, and our success will be ours for the taking.

— Day 204 —

"To not do your best is a failure in itself."

◀   *Matthew 5:48*   ▶

You therefore must be perfect, as your heavenly Father is perfect.

Perfection isn't in the natural order of things.

Not for people, nor for anything that people touch or do.

It's why a good batting average in Major League Baseball is under 300, and only in rare instances have MLB players finished their careers with a perfect average of 1000.

Players can be very successful, even with less than perfect hits. It's doing their best that counts. It's only when they no longer try that they become a failure.

Our journey toward our goal will involve as many misses as hits. Our job is to strive to be as perfect as we can.

We must mold ourselves after our heavenly Father.

It's our goal, although we'll miss the mark much of the time. We only fail if we don't get back up and try once more. If we're doing our best (and not just saying that), we'll reach our goal.

— Day 205 —

"Mistakes will be made. It's standing back up and dusting yourself off that reveals your inner strength."

◁   *1 Corinthians 6:12*   ▷

"All things are lawful for me," but not all things are helpful. "All things are lawful for me," but I will not be enslaved by anything.

Whatever keeps us from our goal is a mistake.

If it isn't helpful in moving us forward, then it's holding us back. It's enslaved us, and we're locked in its chains day and night.

What do you use as your reason for not finding your success? A family member? A lack of education? Inexperience?

These may be valid excuses . . . oh, did you catch that word? The world may accept them as *excuses,* but they've become bindings around our wrists that keep us from what we desire.

We can't afford to be enslaved by anything that holds us back. We need to dust ourselves off and move ahead.

Our future isn't in our chains. It's in our backbone and the things we've cast aside to achieve our goal.

— Day 206 —

"Before you fight tooth and nail for something, make sure it's worth fighting for."

◀   Romans 12:17   ▶

Repay no one evil for evil, but give thought to do what is honorable in the sight of all.

We pay a price for getting things now.

That new car, what are we giving up to own it?

Or our weekends in the city. Is our job performance suffering on Monday?

What benefit are we getting from our part-time job, if our kids don't have us around?

Are we making choices that benefit everyone?

Some things feel good in the moment, but we pay a price that's too high. We wander off the path toward our goal, and it becomes lost.

We honor our commitment to ourselves when we forgo immediate gratification to improve our prospects for our future. Our success will arrive soon enough, and our goal will be ours.

— Day 207 —

"If you want to live your dreams, then you must put forth the necessary effort to achieve them."

◀   *Romans 12:11*   ▶

Do not be slothful in zeal, be fervent in spirit, serve the Lord.

Drive by a youth gymnastics club. Step inside and look at all the kids.

They're working hard to be the best in the world.

They have dreams of Olympic glory and receiving the gold medal.

They are doing whatever it takes to achieve that dream, including hours of practice that wears them down.

Dancers do it, and so do those with musical talent, all because they have a dream.

How much is our dream worth? Hours in preparation? Weekends pounding the pavement? Giving up our vacation or a new car?

Our goal is out there waiting on us. It's time for us to decide what we want. Let's go for it!

— Day 208 —

"Work to do things for the right reason, and you will find the rewards to be far greater. Soon you will find that you won't have to work at doing things for the right reason; it will come naturally."

◀   Hebrews 11:6   ▶

And without faith it is impossible to please him, for whoever would draw near to God must believe that he exists and that he rewards those who seek him.

When training a pet, we can use food as a reward.

The animal will do what we want, but they are doing it for the food. Eventually, that begins to change. We praise them then slowly begin reducing the food.

Their reward becomes our praise.

When we're doing the right thing, sometimes we need people to pat us on the back, because we feel we're being forced to perform. *A treat*, we beg. *A treat for doing a good job*, and we expect to receive a reward.

Eventually, our attitude changes. We do what's right because it's *right*, and not for a reward.

We're on the way to our goal, and it will come *naturally*.

— Day 209 —

"Seek not answers, but rather, the truth."

◀ John 8:32 ▶

And you will know the truth, and the truth will set you free.

Answers change. The most popular color might be green this year and blue the next. Or sugar might be considered healthy this decade and a health risk the next.

We can also skew information to achieve the answers we want. Leave off certain comparisons or only reveal part of the graph, and people will read into it what we want.

Truth is universal. What we know today will be the same tomorrow. It was the same yesterday. It hasn't changed, and it won't change.

Our spiritual and moral truth lies in the person and life of Jesus. We choose to live like Him if we want heaven to be our home.

Reaching our goal involves yet another truth. Our life is our responsibility, and we can make it into what we want it to be. The choice is ours, and we must make our decision today.

— Day 210 —

"Always understand that success is not a measure of wealth or power. It is the measure of achieving your goals, your desires, and your dreams."

◀   3 John 1:2   ▶

Beloved, I pray that all may go well with you and that you may be in good health, as it goes well with your soul.

A river runs from the mountain to the sea.

It has one goal, to reach the ocean. It tumbles down rocky inclines, courses across fertile fields, and eventually pours into the vastness of the blue, to be mixed with all the waters in the world.

The river doesn't worry about bank accounts or investment holdings. They aren't a river's concern. It doesn't measure its success with a financial ruler.

Are we measuring our success with the correct ruler? Money isn't the only one out there.

List every goal you've reached. That's your ruler. Write down the desires you've had fulfilled. Add your dreams that have been realized.

You're getting it. Success is about living. Let's do it well.

— Day 211 —

"Never lose hope, for you don't know what tomorrow may bring."

◀ Romans 15:13 ▶

May the God of hope fill you with all joy and peace in believing, so that by the power of the Holy Spirit you may abound in hope.

Hope is a uniquely human attribute.

Many pets anticipate . . . or look forward to things with the certainty they'll come about. Your dog anticipates your arrival home. Your fish is confident your presence means food will soon appear.

What about when there's nothing to reasonably suggest anything good will happen?

And all evidence says it won't?

That's when humans shine. We find hope, or the faith that things will change for the better, even when there's no proof.

Our hope is the first step in moving toward our goal. We hope, then we determine; we prepare, and then we move into our future and toward our goal. Never lose hope for the future.

— Day 212 —

"True success comes through trusting in the Lord and His Word every day of your life."

◀   Psalm 32:10   ▶

Many are the sorrows of the wicked, but steadfast love surrounds the one who trusts in the LORD.

Trust is defined, literally, as reliance on someone's character, ability, or strength.

It's found in the truth of who they are.

It's when we don't have trust that things begin to go wrong. Our friends fall away. We no longer feel safe in intimacy. Our relationships turn stormy. Our thoughts race, and we see others as deceptive or malevolent, even when we have no evidence.

We can head a world-class business, and without trust, we're miserable. We don't have success. We just have money, and one doesn't equal the other.

Our first step to building trust and moving toward true success is to find something that never changes, something we can count on without pause. Try reading the Bible, a book filled with the faith of a hundred generations. Place your trust in God.

— Day 213 —

"Watch where you step, for you never know whose toes might be there."

◄│   Acts 20:35   │►

In all things I have shown you that by working hard in this way we must help the weak and remember the words of the Lord Jesus, how he himself said, "It is more blessed to give than to receive."

To step on someone's toes, we must get very close to them.

If we get ahead by stepping on someone's toes, then whose feet must they belong to? Our spouse, a business associate, or a neighbor we know well? Probably. Our children, perhaps, or the attendant at the gas station? Certainly.

Good manners are a first-class solution for most situations. Be polite. Smile. Use someone's name. End on a positive note.

Carelessness only creates bruises that take a long time to heal.

Jesus said that it's more blessed to give than to receive. That can mean money, but it also includes our time, our kind words, and our good manners. It means we're aware of who's around us, and we're taking them into consideration. No one should get in our way as we travel our path to success.

— Day 214 —

"Not attempting to reach for the highest level of success imaginable is a failure to do your best."

◀ꞮI   ꞮꞮ *1 Samuel 2:8*   ꞮꞮ▶

He raises up the poor from the dust; he lifts the needy from the ash heap to make them sit with princes and inherit a seat of honor. For the pillars of the earth are the LORD's, and on them he has set the world.

Our goal must always be the next thing.

A Formula 1 driver sees the car just in front of him, and he determines he will pass it.

That's his goal. He's going to overtake that car, however long it takes.

When he's past it, the race isn't over. He sets his sights on the next car, and it becomes his goal. He does this over and over, until he wins the race.

We move from last place to first place one goal at a time. If we rest on our past successes, we'll never achieve a podium finish. We want to sit on the pillars of the earth, and dine with the princes in a seat of honor. Reach for the highest goal, always!

— Day 215 —

"Time is your most valuable resource;
don't let it go to waste."

◀︎   Proverbs 6:9-11   ▶︎

How long will you lie there, O sluggard? When will you arise from
your sleep? A little sleep, a little slumber, a little folding of the
hands to rest, and poverty will come upon you like a robber, and
want like an armed man.

Time-saving devices are a dime a dozen.

Robotic vacuum cleaners, individual hot dog steamers, and coffee pots that turn themselves on and off.

We are hardly forced to do anything, anymore. We can even buy toilet cleaner to hang under the rim. Just flush, and never scrub again.

Who hasn't tried shower spray? They have an automatic version that sprays our shower when we're not there.

What do we do with all that time? Nap? Catch the sun?

Nope. It's time to pursue your goal. Move into the future. Chase your dream until it becomes yours.

— Day 216 —

*"Being honest and trustworthy will take
you further than deceit and disloyalty."*

◀   *1 Corinthians 4:2*   ▶

Moreover, it is required of stewards that they be found trustworthy.

A steward holds a position of power.

It's not what the steward owns but what's under the steward's control. What does the steward hold responsibility for, and does the steward use it well?

Our financial advisors are stewards of our money. We invest it, and they watch over it. If they are trustworthy, we're better for it.

What do we watch over? Our children, our jobs, our churches. We're required to use honesty in all our dealings. It makes the world better.

As we move toward our goal of success, we must carefully consider our actions. What we do affects others. We must not let our influence be a negative one. Our role in our position of power is to improve the world. When we do it well, we'll find our success around the bend.

— Day 217 —

*"Without knowledge, drive, or passion,
you will find success fleeting."*

◁   1 Kings 2:3   ▷

*And keep the charge of the LORD your God, walking in his ways
and keeping his statutes, his commandments, his rules, and his
testimonies, as it is written in the Law of Moses, that you may
prosper in all that you do and wherever you turn.*

Some things are linear.

That means they follow one after another. We can't get them
out of order, or things don't work properly. The pieces of the
puzzle simply won't *fit*.

To find our success, we must have these three things:

1. Knowledge – something gained with experience
2. Drive – an inescapable need or desire
3. Passion – overwhelming conviction

Lasting success won't come without these three things in
place.

Success that lasts requires us to pursue it daily. Start now.

— Day 218 —

"The first and most effective method of teaching is to lead by example."

Philippians 2:3   I▶

Do nothing from rivalry or conceit, but in humility count others more significant than yourselves.

A recent YouTube video showed a puppy afraid to walk down a set of stairs. No amount of pleading convinced the animal.

Then the puppy's owner got on the top step and showed the puppy how it was done, using his hands. The puppy imitated him, one step at a time.

By the bottom third, the puppy had it down and ran the final steps on its own.

We want others to find their success along with us. It's our job to give them support. We do it by getting down to their level, giving them specific instructions, and repeating those instructions until they understand.

We're not out to prove we're better than they are, but to convince them they are as good as us. Let's be encouragers!

— Day 219 —

"Offer support to the struggling, and they will aid you in your rise to success."

◀ *Mark 2:3* ▶

And they came, bringing to him a paralytic carried by four men.

Why do people struggle?

- They let envy consume them.
- They don't stay busy.
- They let problems fester.
- They don't share their feelings.
- They ignore their passion.
- They don't have a balanced relationship.
- They choose to be negative.

Here are some solutions for struggling people: Get your eyes off others. Do something productive. Take care of issues as soon as they happen. Talk to someone. Figure out what you love. Avoid people who don't respect you. Start the day with a positive quote from Success-Speak.

Offer your hand to someone in need, and you'll find success through each other.

— Day 220 —

"Once you begin dwelling in the past, you will find your progress in life will come to a standstill."

◀   *Job 26:10*   ▶

He has inscribed a circle on the face of the waters at the boundary between light and darkness.

Our world turns at a frightful speed, yet no one falls off.

An airplane is held aloft by tenuous air.

They both must keep moving constantly. It's the nature of what they are.

That's us, literally. Our future is always somewhere just in front of us, and that's where our next goal is found. If we stop chasing it, we'll come to a standstill.

Like the earth no longer turning.

Or an airplane falling from the sky.

The past is a DVD that's already been viewed. The images are still there, but watching them over and over is a waste of time. We have our success to chase and our goal to accomplish. Get off the couch. Move forward. Embrace the future.

— Day 221 —

"Cross the line into greed, and you will always achieve less than you desire."

Proverbs 28:25   ▶

A greedy man stirs up strife, but the one who trusts in the LORD will be enriched.

The media portrays success to us in glamorous ways: a large home; sleek cars; maybe a pool, a boat, or a mountain cabin.

Always, always, we see smiles and happy expressions in the media's image of success.

Yet, the truth of it is that wanting too much can slip all too easily into demanding everything. A little makes us want more, and we no longer care how we get it.

In our scramble to get everything, we step on toes, forget the people along the way, and forego the important things.

We lose the happiness.

Our success comes from the relationships we enjoy on the way up. We have them at the top because we didn't lose them along the way. That's true success, and greed just gets in the way.

— Day 222 —

"To truly be successful you must not only take responsibility for your actions but accept them willingly, whether they are positive or negative."

◀   *Matthew 12:37*   ▶

For by your words you will be justified, and by your words you will be condemned.

Stepping up to the plate.

That's baseball jargon, but it means something to the rest of us, too.

It means to take responsibility, to hold the bat and show whether you can hit a home run or not.

Are you ready to play ball or just wearing the uniform?

We can't be blamers. No one appreciates a lazy person. No brag-a-lots, either. None of those allowed. We must have shoulders that can carry what we did, whether it was good or bad.

It's the only way to move into our success. We must toe the line and face the music.

We must accept the responsibility for our actions, positive or negative. Only then will we discover that our goal is at hand.

— Day 223 —

"When you are without a path, success
will escape your grasp."

◀ *James 2:18* ▶

But someone will say, "You have faith and I have works." Show me
your faith apart from your works, and I will show you my faith by
my works.

Our desire for success can't stand alone.

We can't make a goal, post it on the fridge, then spend the next five years in front of the television. We must chase after it. We are to be busy, doing things that will precipitate our success.

Just speaking it isn't enough, if it doesn't change our behavior. Our success-speak must be internalized for it to work.

James said his faith was evident because of his works.

That's how people will know we're on the road to our success. They'll see our goal posted on our fridge, but they'll also see us in preparation, find us actively pursuing goal-oriented objectives, and watch us getting ever closer.

Our path will be clear, because our footsteps will be there.

— Day 224 —

"Step back, observe what went wrong, and make another attempt. Learn this and you can reach your goal."

◀ॻ   Hebrews 1:1-2   ॥▶

Long ago, at many times and in many ways, God spoke to our fathers by the prophets, but in these last days he has spoken to us by his Son, whom he appointed the heir of all things, through whom also he created the world.

A plan that falls through is only a disaster if we let it be.

Instead, we should consider how it can become a stepping stone to lead us somewhere else.

In the financial disaster of 2008, a retired couple lost their nest egg of nearly half-a-million dollars. It was totally gone. They were forced to liquidate their house and all their belongings.

It could have been a disaster. They saw it as an opportunity, purchased a used motor home from their son, and went on the road. Soon they were living in all the exotic places they'd dreamed of and never had the chance to visit.

Life has a way of tossing disasters our way. What we do with them is up to us. Your success is still waiting. Go find it.

— Day 225 —

"Opportunities may slip away. Always be watchful for the next one."

◄‖ *Proverbs 10:5* ‖►

He who gathers in summer is a prudent son, but he who sleeps in harvest is a son who brings shame.

Think of your next opportunity as an ice cube.

You can hold it in your hand, but only for a time. Hold it too long, and it melts through your fingers.

An opportunity is meant to be used. Once it's gone, it's difficult to gather up the water and form it into an ice cube again.

You might say it's impossible.

What's next on your goal list? The must-do part? A college class? Sign up for the next one. A seminar over buying real estate? Register now. Improving your diet? Now, this minute, toss out the bad stuff.

Don't wait. Your opportunity will melt away before the clock strikes noon, and it will be gone, gone, gone.

Find success. Move forward. Make every opportunity count.

— Day 226 —

"Your words will open and close
opportunities in your life."

◀ Mark 5:34 ▶

And [Jesus] said to her, "Daughter, your faith has made you well;
go in peace, and be healed of your disease."

The phrase "You're so special" has a special flair in Southern vernacular. Its meaning is evident in the tone of voice and a drawn-out emphasis on the last word.

You're not special at all, no matter how sweetly it's said.

Yet, in other circumstances, the same phrase relates a tender endearment beyond compare, words from a parent to a child expressing devoted love.

One drives a wedge, and the other binds us together. It's all in how the speaker says the words, but it's also in *how the listener hears them.*

It's the same when we talk to ourselves. We soon begin to believe what we say, even about us.

Use success-speak daily. It will make a difference.

— Day 227 —

"Understand the possibilities, know the consequences, yet don't give in to fear, or your progress will be nil."

◀ Hebrews 12:11 ▶

For the moment all discipline seems painful rather than pleasant, but later it yields the peaceful fruit of righteousness to those who have been trained by it.

Small airports are the domain of prop-driven aircraft.

Two- and four-seat craft litter the tarmac like a child's toys, sparkling in the sun, and ready for a day's enjoyment.

Preparing to fly isn't all fun and games. Every pilot knows the hundred things that can go wrong. Before starting the engine, the pilot must thoroughly inspect the plane, from checking for water in the fuel, to the flaps that direct the craft.

Small airplanes do fall from the sky from time to time. They run out of fuel, the engine chokes and dies, or things don't work.

If the pilot is paralyzed by fear, the aircraft will be grounded. No one will go anywhere. Instead, checks are made, the engine is started, and they are off, trusting in the pilot's expertise.

Preparation is our key. We must move toward our goal.

— Day 228 —

"Believing that something is possible is the first step toward making it a realization."

◀ Daniel 12:3 ▶

And those who are wise shall shine like the brightness of the sky above; and those who turn many to righteousness, like the stars forever and ever.

Most everyone has a mobile phone.

They're ubiquitous in our modern world. We can't go anywhere without seeing them. We use them in our cars and out on the lake. Mountaineers call from Everest to tell the world they've arrived.

The concept started from a science fiction television show that premiered in 1966. We watched, believed cell phones were possible, and we created them.

We can reach to the sky if we believe we can. We can reach any goal, make any level of success ours, and become who we want to be.

We must believe it, first. Then we prepare. Then we act to move into realizing our goal. The time is now!

— Day 229 —

*"Often failure is not a lack of knowledge,
but rather a lack of understanding."*

◀ *Luke 2:52* ▶

*And Jesus increased in wisdom and in stature and in favor with
God and man.*

How wise is a book?

Not very. It just sits there unless we pick it up.

It's packed with knowledge, cover to cover, but the information is no good until we understand what's contained within the pages.

Understanding, combined with wisdom, builds stature and favor with God and man.

We can carry around a book on taking control of the stock market, but unless we understand the information inside, we'll never be a successful broker.

Our preparation for our goal is paramount to achieving it.

Study. Build contacts. Take classes. Prepare. Look for opportunities, then move into your success.

— Day 230 —

"Understanding the obstacles in your life will allow you to overcome the negative effects that the fears, the opposition, and those who would stand against you have upon your life."

◀   Zechariah 4:6   ▶

Then he said to me, "This is the word of the LORD to Zerubbabel: Not by might, nor by power, but by my Spirit, says the LORD of hosts."

There's a tee shirt that says life can be reduced to three things: birth, taxes, and death. The rest? It's all minor.

We must see it that way if we don't want to get bogged down in life. Look at it like this: When we're eighty, and we think back on life, what's the stuff that will count? What will we remember as especially important, the cost of repairing the roof on the lake house, or the summers we enjoyed there with family and friends?

Will the extra cost of our college class be our defining moment, or the promotion we received because of it?

It's all minor, details that fall between the milestones of our lives. We'll be afraid at times and face opposition. People will try to hold us back. It's all inconsequential, when compared to where we're going. Be strong. Be committed. Your success is waiting.

— Day 231 —

"The greatest understanding in the world comes not from knowledge, but from comprehension."

◀   *Job 28:28*   ▶

And he said to man, "Behold, the fear of the Lord, that is wisdom, and to turn away from evil is understanding."

It's like the cartoon lightbulb that appears above a character's head.

Aha! I get it! We read the sudden comprehension in the expression on his face. The knowledge is there, the facts align, and a new idea is born.

It's like a crime show, where the detective sees the facts but doesn't line them up. Then that one detail sparks a transformation, and the answer is there. *Aha! I get it!*

We can have all the facts, but without that *Aha!* moment, we're not moving forward.

Job says that our fear (respect) of the Lord is our wisdom, and when we turn from evil, we have understanding.

Practice Job's words. In comprehension comes our success.

— Day 232 —

"Your success in life is not so much dependent on your intelligence as it is on the passion and effort you are willing to put forward to achieve your goals."

◀︎   2 Peter 1:5-8   ▶︎

For this very reason, make every effort to supplement your faith with virtue, and virtue with knowledge, and knowledge with self-control, and self-control with steadfastness, and steadfastness with godliness, and godliness with brotherly affection, and brotherly affection with love. For if these qualities are yours and are increasing, they keep you from being ineffective or unfruitful in the knowledge of our Lord Jesus Christ.

Stephen Hawking has an undeniable passion for physics. He's proven himself to be one of the greatest thinkers of the modern age.

Yet, he's a man trapped in his own body. It takes great effort for him to communicate with the outside world.

His unquenchable effort has been the core of his achievement. If he'd quit trying, we'd have none of his brilliance recorded for posterity.

Practice speaking success-speak. Give effort. Have passion. Step out. Find success. Reach a goal. Make your future yours.

— Day 233 —

"Success can often include wealth, power, and influence, but that's not the case for everyone."

◄ Proverbs 22:29 ►

Do you see a man skillful in his work? He will stand before kings; he will not stand before obscure men.

Mike Rowe in *Dirty Jobs* celebrated skilled workers.

Not just those in fancy uniforms, either. He showed that success comes in all shapes, sizes, and degrees of dirt.

If we've set a goal, moved forward to achieve it, and enjoy what we're doing, we can be covered with grime and still feel successful in our line of work.

Even if we're not rich. Or powerful. Or wield influence among the influential.

Our success is very personal. What's important to us? What goal have we set? Have we reached it?

The important thing is to be the best we can be at whatever we've chosen to pursue. When we are, we will stand out and be noticed, receive our acclaim, and stand before kings.

— Day 234 —

"Search for what you desire, be thankful for what you have, and work for what you need."

Colossians 3:17   ▸

And whatever you do, in word or deed, do everything in the name of the Lord Jesus, giving thanks to God the Father through him.

Our lives fall into three categories.

1. Ownership – where we are in life
2. Needs – things we don't have but that are vital to our existence
3. Desires – things we don't need but want

One of these we have. The other two we don't. What we don't possess is what drives us to better ourselves.

Our first step is to accept where we are and to be thankful for what we've got. Yes, for our house, even if it's small. For our messy children and even for our job that doesn't pay well.

Next, decide what's vital and work for it. Only then pursue what we desire. We must prioritize our lives, never forgetting to appreciate what we already have. Today is part of our success. It's a journey as much as it is a destination.

— Day 235 —

"Everything you really need is within your grasp."

◀   *Matthew 6:25*   ▶

Therefore I tell you, do not be anxious about your life, what you will eat or what you will drink, nor about your body, what you will put on. Is not life more than food, and the body more than clothing?

Worry.

It doesn't resolve our problems, but it sure gives us something to do. We can wring our hands, lie awake at night, and consume lots of antacids for our stomach.

Why worry? Are we about to starve? Will the house be repossessed tomorrow? Are we truly about to be hauled away to the poor house?

Write down where you are. Put your needs in one category, and your wants in another. Don't get them confused.

Let today be today. Tomorrow is your goal. You're on the road to your success. Your desires will come to you, if you internalize Success-Speak and stay the course.

— Day 236 —

"Acquiring what you desire is not a prerequisite to happiness."

◀   *2 Timothy 3:2*   ▶

For people will be lovers of self, lovers of money, proud, arrogant, abusive, disobedient to their parents, ungrateful, [and] unholy.

Babies are cute. They are also very self-centered. A baby's world extends about as far as its fingertips.

It wants what it wants, and it needs what it needs, and it doesn't consider other people in the process.

We can't be babies all our lives. We must grow out of our self-centered lifestyle. We can't demand the world to pay attention to *me, me, me* any longer.

Paul says he's learned to be content in whatever state he's in (Philippians 4:11). If the money's rolling in, he's content. If he's forced to downsize, he's content. If the business is doing well . . .

You get it.

It's time to grow up. Our happiness can be now, while we're preparing for success, as we're moving forward toward our goal.

— Day 237 —

"The process of achieving what you desire can bring you joy."

▲ 1 Peter 1:8 ▶

Though you have not seen him, you love him. Though you do not now see him, you believe in him and rejoice with joy that is inexpressible and filled with glory.

Anticipation is the name of the game. It's almost better than reaching our goal.

Why?

When we *anticipate,* we can let our *imagination* run wild.

Imagine when you first wanted children. You pictured hugs, happy smiles, and beautiful birthday parties. You got all that, along with diapers, temper tantrums, and rows of sleepless nights.

You still love your child, even more after he or she arrives, but the reality isn't quite what we imagined. Our anticipation brought us joy even as we waited for our love to be complete.

Our success goal is the same. It will be wonderful to achieve, but the process of bringing it about is joyful, also.

— Day 238 —

"When the core of who you are suffers to further wealth or power, then success has escaped you."

◀   *Matthew 11:28*   ▶

Come to me, all who labor and are heavy laden, and I will give you rest.

Turn on a flashlight. It will run down eventually. The brighter the beam, the faster it goes down.

Batteries need recharged. They need to be plugged in once in a while, even the most powerful and longest lasting.

How's your battery doing? Pursuing wealth or power is one of the fastest drains on our internal battery of anything out there. We can get so caught up in it that we don't take time to replenish what we need to survive.

Our success becomes hollow, and we no longer enjoy what we've achieved.

Our time to recharge is here. Rethink that goal. Adjust your priorities. Let your soul recharge. Rest up to take on your next challenge. This is your opportunity to move forward once again and find the success that nearly slipped away.

— Day 239 —

"Just because somebody knows the 'right' things to do in life, does not mean they will act on them."

◀ Romans 14:23 ▶

But whoever has doubts is condemned if he eats, because the eating is not from faith. For whatever does not proceed from faith is sin.

There's a reason we give new drivers a beginner's license and force them to drive with an adult in the car.

They may have attended all the classes, and they may know all the material, but until they *practice behind the wheel,* they're not safe to be around.

In an emergency, they will respond by reflex, and theirs aren't honed yet. Their responses must become automatic, something beyond question, a thing they do without thinking.

Our journey to success needs the same automatic reactions, the right ones, the choices that allow us to continue along the path to our goal. If an emergency causes us to veer off the road, we'll crash our well-laid-out plans, and we'll be forced to back up and start over.

Be smart. Find a mentor. Practice before getting on the road.

— Day 240 —

"Live your life for what you want to be."

◀   *Galatians 5:16*   ▶

But I say, walk by the Spirit, and you will not gratify the desires of the flesh.

Put a halter on an unbroken horse. The animal will fight to get free. The halter limits its freedom. Yet, a well-trained horse is a pleasure, and it bonds with its handler in a special way.

We are that unbroken horse. We fight against the rules that limit our freedom. Gluttony. Drugs. Sensual desires. We want them all.

Yet, a person who lives a well-managed life, avoids disreputable behavior, and sets a good example for others can build respect from family, friends, and business associates. Self-centeredness goes out the window. The desires of the flesh, stamped out. It's how we reach our goal.

Our harness is the Spirit of God, our handler is Jesus, and our journey leads us toward our goal. What do you want to be? Decide now. Your decision can lead you to your success.

— Day 241 —

"The deeper you dig your hole, the harder it is to climb out. Honesty is our ladder to success."

◀   2 Corinthians 8:21   ▶

For we aim at what is honorable not only in the Lord's sight but also in the sight of man.

It's illegal to dig in the sand at beaches in Florida.

In 52 cases of sand-hole collapse in the U.S. and three other countries, according to an ABC News report, 31 people died.

They couldn't climb out, and without air, they only had a few minutes to survive.

What's our hole in the sand? Fudging office reports to gain favor? Creative accounting to lower our income tax bill? Hiding our searches on the Internet to cover our tracks?

We have a ladder to exit our hole: 1. Honesty. 2. Being truthful in all that we say and do. 3. Striving to stand before God as we wish to appear before men.

We can move forward when we quit digging our hole and climb out. We exit on the rungs of honesty and aim for our goal.

— Day 242 —

"Undertaking a decision without understanding the consequences of your action is a risky proposition."

◀ *Proverbs 25:26* ▶

Like a muddied spring or a polluted fountain is a righteous man who gives way before the wicked.

NASCAR rules are in place for a reason.

- Cars are required to display numbers on doors and roofs.
- A single car must be used from the practice run through the end of the race.
- Engine changes are prohibited during a race weekend.
- The driver who starts the race earns all the purse money, even if a replacement driver fills in.

These rules level the playing field. Break the rules, any of the rules, and face stiff penalties. The teams and drivers must make good decisions or risk forfeiting their qualification.

How's your race toward your goal going? There are rules in place there, too. Preparation. Patience. Action. Get to it!

— Day 243 —

*"The more you improve your knowledge,
the greater the value and number of
opportunities that will become available
to you."*

◀   *John 9:4*   ▶

*We must work the works of him who sent me while it is day; night
is coming, when no one can work.*

Harvesting fruit is an exacting process.

Pull it from the plant too early, and we risk losing the sweetness that makes it desirable. Too late, and it's on its way to ruin.

We must study to learn the signs the harvest is imminent. Otherwise, our only choice is the garbage bin.

Our chance for success also has a door that opens and closes. We must seize it during the day, when the light of opportunity streams through. Once the darkness of night closes the door, our uplifting prospect for the future will be gone.

The more we study the maturity of our fruit, the greater its value on the market. We must recognize when our skills are ripe for change. Once the door opens, we must be ready to step through. Learn while you can. Move now.

— Day 244 —

"Your mind is the greatest resource you can own."

◀   Philippians 4:8   ▶

Finally, brothers, whatever is true, whatever is honorable, whatever is just, whatever is pure, whatever is lovely, whatever is commendable, if there is any excellence, if there is anything worthy of praise, think about these things.

If we own a quality car, we maintain it with diligence, or it becomes worthless.

A fruit orchard? Netting protects the fruit, and smudge pots prevent freezing.

So why let our best resource go to rack and ruin?

It's through our mind that we take advantage of our opportunity for success. We must have the knowledge to prepare and wisdom to know when to move into our future.

Are you still a couch potato? Is your phone stuck on social media? Or are you focused on improving your skills to advance toward your goal? Without building your mind, your efforts will be defeated, and you'll be stuck in the muck of the past forever.

— Day 245 —

"Standing up and doing what needs to be done is the only way you can truly make a difference."

◀︎   **Ecclesiastes 12:13-14**   ▶︎

The end of the matter; all has been heard. Fear God and keep his commandments, for this is the whole duty of man. For God will bring every deed into judgment, with every secret thing, whether good or evil.

It's the cutting-edge innovator who earns the awards.

The first-place athlete gets into the record books, not the rest of the competitors.

Who do we remember, the first man to walk on the moon, or the second, third, or fourth?

The deeds we perform now are judged by the world in real time. Pablo Picasso invented cubism, a new style of painting, and no one could steal his acclaim. Anyone can paint in the abstract expressionist style of Jackson Pollock, but only a Pollock will bring the $140 million paid for a single work in 2017.

It's your time to make your mark. Do what's you. Be inimitable, cutting edge, and come in first place. Chase your goal.

— Day 246 —

"Do not fear the unknown; occasionally it will bring you a good surprise."

◀   Luke 1:35   ▶

And the angel answered her, "The Holy Spirit will come upon you, and the power of the Most High will overshadow you; therefore the child to be born will be called holy—the Son of God.

Mary, the mother of Jesus, was in a brand-new place.

It was a path no one had traveled before, one that could bring shame on her and her future husband.

She trusted in the unknown situation, finding her faith in the words of an angel, and the greatest religious figure in the world was born.

What unknown are you facing? You've never been to college? That can be frightening. Moving to the city? It boggles the mind.

Change is always unknown. That's why it's called change. We must break out, take a chance, and forge ahead.

Our goal is out there. We're headed to success. Fear is out the door. Excitement rules the day. Run toward your future now.

— Day 247 —

"The easy path grants minimal rewards."

Matthew 7:14   ▶

For the gate is narrow and the way is hard that leads to life, and those who find it are few.

We can't use the 5-pound weights and win the body-builder award.

Our walk to the mailbox won't prepare us for a 26-mile marathon.

Flipping through a magazine on the lifestyles of the rich and the famous won't put us in their sphere.

Work earns rewards. Do a little work, and get a little reward. Burn the candle a little brighter, and the flame gets hotter.

The more we chase our goal, the closer it will become. Want a bakery? Begin cooking and sharing now. Opening a new shop? Begin researching commercial rental rates. That college degree? Learn the registration requirements.

One person controls your future. You. Get started.

— Day 248 —

"Do you doubt the words of those near you? Can you trust the people you associate with? You become like the people you are around."

◀   *Psalm 118:8*   ▶

It is better to take refuge in the LORD than to trust in man.

Our reputation is the best thing we own.

Celebrities regularly lose financial endorsements due to poorly phrased comments or jokes. Christian Dior disbanded their relationship with a prominent actress when she blamed a devastating earthquake on China's bad "karma." AFLAC did the same with a well-known actor who joked about the tsunami that hit Japan in 2011.

Companies no longer wanted to be associated with them.

When people around us have a bad reputation, that rubs off on us. If we don't become like them (and often we do mimic their bad behavior), people think we do, and our opportunities to reach our goal evaporate.

Let's aim for a higher standard. When we adhere to Godly standards, we've elevated ourselves and are aimed toward success. Our future is in our sights. Ready, set, go!

— Day 249 —

*"Wisdom and patience go hand-in-hand
with success."*

◀   *Luke 21:15*   ▶

*For I will give you a mouth and wisdom, which none of your
adversaries will be able to withstand or contradict.*

Walk on a cement sidewalk before it's cured, and you'll leave footprints.

The surface is affected permanently. Once the cement hardens, there's little option but to live with the results of our impatience.

A smart person walks around the wet cement while it's curing. It's called using wisdom . . . and showing patience.

We can't rush our goal into place. We must be ready. It's like putting in a grape orchard. We don't get juice the first year, or the second. We must be patient until our third year. If we dig up the plants and toss them out, we've wasted our time and money.

Set up your milestones on the way to your success. Embrace them. Celebrate each small victory. Your greater goal is on the way. Be patient. Show wisdom. Be ready for your success.

— Day 250 —

"You may feel overwhelmed, but success comes with determination."

◀︎ Psalm 23:4 ▶︎

Even though I walk through the valley of the shadow of death, I will fear no evil, for you are with me; your rod and your staff, they comfort me.

At times, life happens too fast.

We're on an F-1 track, surrounded by high-powered cars traveling at great speed, and our brakes are out.

We're flying into a wall, and there's nowhere to go.

F-1 cars are built with crumple zones. The car can disintegrate and still protect the driver. Nomex suits shield the occupants from burning fuel.

Fatalities are rare on the F-1 circuit.

Sometimes we must trust in our preparation, tuck our head, and let life happen. Then we climb out of the mess and move back into the race.

Don't give up. Success is coming. Make another effort.

— Day 251 —

"Watch out for the agendas and desires of others. The path to your success is your responsibility."

◂ *Matthew 26:41* ▸

Watch and pray that you may not enter into temptation. The spirit indeed is willing, but the flesh is weak.

Wooded paths are beautiful.

Like to jog? We can enjoy nature and get our exercise, too.

It's the roots and stones we must watch for. They can trip us up, and down we go, nose to the sand.

On our path to success, we will be tempted to go along to get along, to pursue avenues that aren't within our venue.

They'll take us off course, and we'll lose sight of our goal.

It's up to us to watch every step and to avoid the roots and stones along the way. We can't let other people dictate our path, or we'll be distracted and down.

Our success is up to us. Our goal is firmly fixed in our mind, not anyone else's. We are the ones with the determination to get there. No one can hold us back. We are champions of our cause.

— Day 252 —

*"Step into the possibilities that come your
way and don't allow them to go unused."*

◀   *Luke 6:38*   ▶

*Give, and it will be given to you. Good measure, pressed down,
shaken together, running over, will be put into your lap. For with
the measure you use it will be measured back to you.*

Luke 6:38 is often quoted to espouse prosperity. If we give
money, we'll get money in return.

It's much more than that.

If we invest our time and energy in the opportunities that
come our way, we'll get results.

Lots of results.

The harder we work, the greater our results will be.

The opposite side of the coin is true, also. If we let the
opportunity pass us by, we're receive no benefit at all.

And we can't blame anyone else.

Jump with both feet. Work hard. Be patient. Expect success.

— Day 253 —

"Watch for and understand the potential consequences of your words. Even a harmless comment or a small quip can do great damage."

◀   *Colossians 3:8*   ▶

But now you must put them all away: anger, wrath, malice, slander, and obscene talk from your mouth.

The optimal ratio for what we say is five to one.

We should make five positive remarks for every criticism we feel necessary.

You've done good work. This color is an excellent choice. What a great meal! I appreciate you mowing the grass. Wow, you cleaned the car.

I see you tracked in dirt.

5-to-1. How many of us do it?

Then we get into gossip, careless remarks in the workplace, or spiteful digs.

We don't know the harm we've done. We must focus on the positive and determine that our words will always accentuate the good we see in others. Be upbeat. Find the good. Move forward.

— Day 254 —

"Stand by what you know, hold your ground with the facts; do not be drawn away from the truths in your life."

◀   Luke 21:1-4   ▶

Jesus looked up and saw the rich putting their gifts into the offering box, and he saw a poor widow put in two small copper coins. And he said, "Truly, I tell you, this poor widow has put in more than all of them. For they all contributed out of their abundance, but she out of her poverty put in all she had to live on."

Faith.

Kindness, generosity, and caring for others.

The Golden Rule says to do unto others as you would have them do unto you. (Matthew 7:12)

It must be the core of who we are, and we can't let anyone take that truth away from us. We must stand by our convictions, our focus on our goal, and who we are.

The widow in Luke was generous to the point of giving all she had. We must commit everything to our goal if we want to succeed. Money. Time. Relationships. We can hold nothing back, or everything will hold us back. Our goal is in our sights.

— Day 255 —

"If you are doing something that would feel shameful if it were to become public, it's probably something you shouldn't be doing."

◀   1 Corinthians 6:9-10   ▶

Or do you not know that the unrighteous will not inherit the kingdom of God? Do not be deceived: [those who behave shamefully] will [not] inherit the kingdom of God.

Our elected officials should be transparent.

Open records acts offer access to public documents.

We have an obligation to be upfront, to be in private as we appear in public.

People are outraged when they find out a public figure says one thing to them and then does the opposite in private.

How will our future employers see us?

How about the people who review our Internet history? Our phone logs? Our family time or our church attendance? Our charity donations?

When success comes our way, it all matters. Live a clean life. Be as you appear. Let nothing distract from your goal.

— Day 256 —

"No obstacle is too great to overcome, but you must ask yourself if the cost to overcome the obstacle is worth the price."

Judges 16:25   ▶

And when their hearts were merry, they said, "Call Samson, that he may entertain us." So they called Samson out of the prison, and he entertained them. They made him stand between the pillars.

Sampson had all the nation of the Philistines arrayed against him.

He'd been captured, his eyes removed, and his arms and legs bound in chains. He was a man out of options.

Then came his chance. God opened an opportunity. It would cost Sampson his life, but to him, it was worth the cost.

Sampson broke the pillars and took his enemy with him.

What price are you asked to pay for success? What does your goal require of you? Is it worth it? Even if it costs you everything? Working nights? College classes? A student loan? Pounding the pavement to drum up financial backers?

It's your dream. Step into it and find success!

— Day 257 —

"Knowing what you're up against will allow you to unpin yourself from the wall of deceit, failure, restraint, and fear."

◀ *1 Corinthians 3:18* ▶

Let no one deceive himself. If anyone among you thinks that he is wise in this age, let him become a fool that he may become wise.

Blinders on a horse allow it to run a race without distractions.

Owners and riders know that focus is key to a podium finish. If our attention gets just a little off, it can make the difference between first place and second or third.

Distractions we need to avoid are:

- Deceit – people who are dishonest
- Failure – remembering previous slip-ups
- Restraint – hesitation at taking risks
- Fear – worry that we might not succeed

We must scope out our competition, then slip on our blinders. Our only focus is success.

We find wisdom when we tune out the extraneous. If it's useless to our success, we don't need it in our life.

— Day 258 —

"Knowing the why can be just as important as understanding the how."

◀   *Exodus 3:14*   ▶

God said to Moses, "I AM WHO I AM." And he said, "Say this to the people of Israel, 'I AM has sent me to you.'"

Two neighbors cook roasts each Sunday for lunch. The young daughter returns from a Sunday visit next door to ask her mother why Mrs. Smith cuts the ends off her roast.

When questioned, Mrs. Smith says it's the way her mother always did it. She calls her mother who explains why.

"My pan was too small. The roast wouldn't fit."

What roast are we still cutting just because "that's the way it's done"?

We can find our direction in God, who tells us he's the "I am who I am." When we focus on the Lord, we'll understand His place in our lives, and the path to our goal will crystalize in front of us.

Understand your purpose. Find your path. Begin now.

— Day 259 —

*"Live out your own definition of success—
not somebody else's."*

◀ Acts 11:23 ▶

When he came and saw the grace of God, he was glad, and he exhorted them all to remain faithful to the Lord with steadfast purpose.

Culture is a strange thing. When we're part of it, it's hard not to become entangled in it.

The nature of culture is that it puts peer pressure on us, trying to force us to become like everyone else.

We must ask ourselves this question: Is that where we want to go? A big house, a boat, three cars, and a corner office? Is that the only definition of success?

Do we also find the grace of God in our plan for success? It comprises forgiveness for wrongs, second chances, shared wealth, and a place of promised security.

Our success must be better than just the corner office the world so admires. Our success must involve the people we're with.

— Day 260 —

"If an opportunity comes your way, you must take it and use it immediately."

Ecclesiastes 9:10   ▶

Whatever your hand finds to do, do it with your might, for there is no work or thought or knowledge or wisdom in Sheol, to which you are going.

We only have today.

In 1963, President John Kennedy was poised to change the world. He led the most powerful country in existence. His plans were interrupted by a sniper's bullet.

In 1999, John Kennedy, Jr. was a rising political star. He was on his way to his cousin's wedding when his private plane disappeared into the ocean.

Tomorrow isn't assured. Reach out and grab the opportunities that come along. Step forward with Success-Speak.

Today's your time. It's your moment to shine.

Make your preparations to move ahead. College. Social connections. Phone calls. Practice, practice, practice. It's now.

— Day 261 —

"Avoid the things that would divert you from your goal, for they will only become obstacles on your path to success."

◀   *Matthew 24:6*   ▶

And you will hear of wars and rumors of wars. See that you are not alarmed, for this must take place, but the end is not yet.

We tend to listen to everything.

It comes in one ear and sticks, when it needs to go out the other.

"You don't have the skills."

"Only a hundred down, and you can drive it home!"

"Must-see new show, tonight at eleven."

These are all distractions. Things that will keep us from our success.

We'll stumble over them on the way to our goal.

We decide our path. It's up to us to take the correct classes, study the appropriate literature, meet the right people, and maneuver past the obstacles strewn in our way. It's our choice.

— Day 262 —

"Never head into a situation with the attitude, 'I'm going to try.' Always enter a situation with, 'I will succeed.'"

◀   *Matthew 5:16*   ▶

In the same way, let your light shine before others, so that they may see your good works and give glory to your Father who is in heaven.

Get up early one morning.

That's right, while it's still dark. Climb out of bed, sleepy-head. Get outside and catch the sunrise.

Here's the thing about seeing the dawn. When the sun breaks across the horizon, it never peeks over the trees, then says, "I just can't do it."

The sun flashes across the morning every time. Under the clouds, over the clouds, behind the clouds, it's there.

Our success is the morning sun rising to greet the world. We can't peek over the horizon and think, maybe not today.

It's our time. Morning has arrived.

If our preparation is in place, we're ready. Our path is assured. It's up to us to step out and achieve our goal.

— Day 263 —

"Investments are like water. If you leave them exposed, they will evaporate."

◀   *Jeremiah 29:7*   ▶

But seek the welfare of the city where I have sent you into exile, and pray to the LORD on its behalf, for in its welfare you will find your welfare.

Banking scams. Identity theft. Online accounts hacked.

Watch out, watch out. We must pay attention, or all our hard work will come undone.

Our investments are more than just money. We invest our time, our emotions, and our relationships. We must work to keep them safe, so that they can help us prosper in the future.

If we ignore them, they will suffer.

Jeremiah says to seek the welfare of our city of exile. For us, that means we attend to our preparations for success. We watch our financial accounts to ensure our funds are adequate. We strive for patience, a good attitude, and a trusting relationship with friends, family, and coworkers. When we do, we'll be prepared when our opportunity comes around.

— Day 264 —

"Do not survive only by what is given to you. Reach out and achieve your desires."

◀ **Revelation 3:21** ▶

The one who conquers, I will grant him to sit with me on my throne, as I also conquered and sat down with my Father on his throne.

Reaching toward our goal is like a man heading up a mountain. The summit is obscured by clouds, the path is steep, and at times, he grows short of breath.

He asks himself what he's doing. He has safety among family and friends below, and what's ahead is only a dream.

Then he closes his eyes and his goal appears to him as real as the path at his feet. He can picture it in his mind. He's reenergized.

What we already possess, no matter the security it gives us, can't satisfy our need for success. We must keep our goal in our mind's eye at all times.

When we reach the summit, we'll be conquerors, victors on our path to success. Take the next step. Move ahead.

— Day 265 —

*"Don't expect to achieve your goal if
you're not willing to work toward it."*

◀ *Ezra 10:4* ▶

Arise, for it is your task, and we are with you; be strong and do it.

A steam engine has one purpose, to move a piston.

It's that moving piston that gets the work done. To get it going, we must light a fire, heat the boiler, and continually stoke the flames.

One more thing: We must grease the piston from time to time. It takes a lot of work, but we get out what we put in.

We're the ones driving our steam engine toward our goal. It's up to us to light the fire and stoke the flames. It's our duty to grease the piston.

Only then will our success machine get us to our goal.

We see people's lives littered with rusty steam engines. It was too much work for them to continue, and their goals are still out there somewhere, unrealized.

Our task is today. Arise. The Lord is with us all the way.

— Day 266 —

*"When you step on the course for success,
your path will carry you to your goal."*

◀   Proverbs 14:23   ▶

In all toil there is profit, but mere talk tends only to poverty.

Moving sidewalks at airports are wonders.

All we do is step on, and we are transported to our destination.

Here's the tricky part. For some people, it can be precarious to take the first step. One foot is still on stationary concrete, and the other is in motion. What if they fall?

It's the second step that resolves the problem. Once they're committed, fully and totally, they can go with the flow, letting the sidewalk carry them along.

If they never step out, their goal will always be somewhere in the distance, and they'll never achieve it.

What have you checked off on your Success-Speak list for today? What goal of yours is in hand? Is the bed made? Did you call and schedule an interview? Celebrate and move forward.

— Day 267 —

"Determine not just to expand your knowledge but to better understand the knowledge you already have."

◀   Acts 1:8   ▶

But you will receive power when the Holy Spirit has come upon you, and you will be my witnesses in Jerusalem and in all Judea and Samaria, and to the end of the earth.

Knowledge equals power. It's using the knowledge that's the issue. We must know how to apply it before we get the power.

The disciples in Acts 1:8 received their power from the Holy Spirit, and they spread the gospel to the end of the earth.

Achieving our goal requires that same leap from knowledge to power. We know what our goal is, we've planned how to get there, and now we need a mentor.

The disciples' mentor was the Holy Spirit.

We find our mentor in an expert in our chosen field. A teacher, an architect, or a master cabinet builder. Set up an interview. Have a discussion. See if you can call back if you have further questions. Use this opportunity to move a step closer to your goal.

— Day 268 —

*"Success that harms your personal life,
your family, or your spirituality in the
guise of chasing money isn't true success."*

2 Corinthians 4:4   ▶

*In their case the god of this world has blinded the minds of the
unbelievers, to keep them from seeing the light of the gospel of the
glory of Christ, who is the image of God.*

Australia's Great Western Woodlands is the largest intact temperate woodland in the world. It's rich in iron and other minerals. Mining companies have proposed stepping in to strip the resources from the land. It could make them a fortune, but at what cost to this pristine and environmentally sensitive area?

Our success in life can't be at the expense of the really important things. Our personal life, are we willing to give up that? Or our family? What if we lose them? Or, and this is the important one, our relationship with God?

Is potential wealth worth the price we might pay?

Sometimes we need the blinders on, so we can focus on our goal. Occasionally we need to look around to make sure we're not leaving anyone behind.

— Day 269 —

"You have two paths before you. The arduous one over the mountain provides great rewards, or the short and easy path gives minimal rewards. Which do you choose?"

◀   Isaiah 35:8   ▶

And a highway shall be there, and it shall be called the Way of Holiness; the unclean shall not pass over it. It shall belong to those who walk on the way; even if they are fools, they shall not go astray.

Deposit $100 into an investment account. Leave it a while.

Even if it gives you 100 percent return, you've only made $100. It was a small risk, and you only get a small return.

Put $10,000 into that same account. Now you've built yourself the potential for a return a hundred times greater than the first. You also carry more risk, in case you lose it all.

Our investments in our future work the same way. Do we want a certificate of completion, or a four-year degree? One is over quickly, while the other requires serious commitment.

Or our marriage. Give up at the first argument, or stick together long enough that we understand one another?

We decide what we want, a little or a lot. It's up to us.

— Day 270 —

"The act of betrayal can be agonizing and is one of the worst possible feelings. True success accompanies sincerity, truth, and loyalty."

Jeremiah 12:6   ▶

For even your brothers and the house of your father, even they have dealt treacherously with you; they are in full cry after you; do not believe them, though they speak friendly words to you.

A pyramid scheme is an investment strategy that milks funds from new investors to repay the early ones.

When it collapses (and it always does), people are betrayed. They can lose vast sums of money.

We want, instead, a secured investment, one truthfully presented by a sincere investment counselor, that will earn our loyalty.

Our success must be of the second sort, and it *is* an investment. We invest vast quantities of our emotions, our time, our relationships, and our future into our goal, and we must make sure it's a sound one.

We must test our plans to ensure they are sound. We must prove our goal. We must be certain. Then we step into success.

— Day 271 —

"The one who waits, the one with patience, often receives the greatest reward."

◀   Psalm 33:20-22   ▶

Our soul waits for the LORD; he is our help and our shield. For our heart is glad in him, because we trust in his holy name. Let your steadfast love, O LORD, be upon us, even as we hope in you.

A good chef knows something about timing.

She can't pull her soufflé out of the oven until it's perfectly done. If she's early, even by a bit, she'll lose that fluffy texture that makes it appealing.

Our journey to our goal is equally precise. When the door for opportunity opens, it's time to move through. We can't force it open, and if we wait too long, it will close again.

We must have the patience for the timing to be just right.

Don't worry that you're still in school and a friend is already earning a paycheck. It's not your time. Stick to your plan, step by step, checking off one box at a time.

You'll reach your goal, and the timing will be perfect for you.

— Day 272 —

"Your path may seem to be fading right in front of your eyes while everything slips from your grasp. Rather than give up, refocus on your goals."

◀   *Proverbs 4:25*   ▶

Let your eyes look directly forward, and your gaze be straight before you.

Rain at night does strange things to highways.

The water covers the road, and the striping seems to disappear.

The striping isn't gone, it's just lost in the glare. We can turn on our fog (or driving) lights, and the lower and brighter beams will reveal what was there all along.

When we've lost sight of our goal, it hasn't gone anywhere. The rain's gotten in the way. Circumstances have blocked it, and our feet have difficulty finding the path.

We need to flip on our fog lights. We can refocus our determination to reach our goal.

Rain doesn't last forever. If we keep moving forward, we'll discover our path once again.

— Day 273 —

"Never forget to say thank you."

◀   *Psalm 136:1*   ▶

Give thanks to the LORD, for he is good, for his steadfast love endures forever.

Gratitude makes us healthier. Seriously. We get:

- Better behaved teens at school
- A brighter outlook on life
- Higher grades in school
- Better relationships
- More productive sleep
- A healthier heart
- An improved immune system

Gratitude also improves our job prospects, is good for team morale, and helps us feel better about ourselves.

Say thank you. Soon you'll begin to mean it. It'll become part of your day. You'll notice the difference. It'll boost your job performance, help you focus on your goal, and carry you forward toward your success.

— Day 274 —

"If you are not careful, lazy people will begin to influence your goals and objectives."

◀   *1 Corinthians 15:33*   ▶

Do not be deceived: "Bad company ruins good morals."

Put a soft orange into a basket freshly picked from the tree.

At first, things will be fine. Our new harvest will slough off the debilitating effects of the overripe fruit without any apparent ill effect.

A short time in, the damage begins to appear. The soft orange turns, develops signs of rot, and the fresh oranges around it soften.

Our only option is to toss out the rotten fruit before it ruins the entire basket.

Laziness is the rot that deflects us from our goal. It spreads when we're too close to it. It's vital we spend our time with industrious, effective people. They become our example and help us build similar skills.

Keep a plan. Know the steps. Avoid distractions. Succeed.

— Day 275 —

"Stick to the path you have chosen and do not falter."

◀   *Luke 2:22*   ▶

And when the time came for their purification according to the Law of Moses, they brought him up to Jerusalem to present him to the Lord.

Luke 2:22 relates one small part of the life of Jesus.

Its effect is huge. Joseph and Mary were raising the most impactful child ever brought into the world. Jesus was the embodiment of God come to offer salvation to the world.

Yet, he was still a child.

Joseph and Mary must have wanted to hold onto the human side of Jesus, yet they followed through on the promise given to Mary. They knew their son belonged to God, and they returned Him to the Father.

Our path can force us to make hard decisions. It can seem easier to take a side road. We want the quick success rather than the one that requires patience and preparation. We must maintain our determination and focus on our goal.

— Day 276 —

"Be observant. You never know how long until your next opportunity will appear."

◀   Matthew 13:17   ▶

For truly, I say to you, many prophets and righteous people longed to see what you see, and did not see it, and to hear what you hear, and did not hear it.

A road trip can be a fun family treat.

See America, up close and personal! Travel her highways! Experience what this great land is all about!

The reality is lots of restroom breaks and lonely stretches of roadway where we see nothing at all.

When we're on the road, we must take our opportunities when they come. We can't manufacture fast food joints and restrooms out of thin air. *Rest Stop 14 Miles.* The scenic junctions are even harder to find.

There are opportunities on our path to success. We can't always plan them, but we can be observant and take advantage of them when they appear. *Opportunity Coming Up.* It's what we're looking for. Take advantage of it today.

— Day 277 —

"Always be respectful toward those who come against you; they are often the ones who need it the most."

Romans 12:14 I▶

Bless those who persecute you; bless and do not curse them.

Respect is a practical decision.

It lifts us up and displays us as the better person.

Life is a team effort. Reaching our goal requires us to work together. People who challenge us are as in need of our assistance as we are of theirs.

In a business environment, respect improves the sharing of knowledge, reduces stress, and elevates employee engagement toward company goals.

Respect also creates a fair environment, one that enables us to achieve at an optimal level.

Our respectful attitude creates a bridge that allows us to remain connected, even when we feel slighted. It helps us see our conflict from our opponents' viewpoint, work through our conflict, and move ahead. Choose respect for your success.

— Day 278 —

"Even if what you say seems innocuous right now, will it still be so harmless ten, twenty, or even thirty years from now? Choose your words carefully."

Ephesians 4:29   ▶

Let no corrupting talk come out of your mouths, but only such as is good for building up, as fits the occasion, that it may give grace to those who hear.

How many times have we wished we could back up and start over?

Educators get to do that every September. Last year's struggles are gone, lessons aren't yet presented, and we have a new class of smiling students.

Our stumbles from the year before can be forgotten. They've moved on to the next grade.

That's fine until we recognize the sibling of last year's troublemaker. Harsh words we've let slip from the previous year are likely to return in every parent conference. If they've festered, they'll be worse the second time around.

Our kind words can come back, also. When we treat others well, they'll support us, and we'll reach our goal faster than ever.

— Day 279 —

"If you really want something, you must attempt every possible avenue of success that is morally acceptable, no matter how exhausting, humiliating, or unpleasant."

◀   *Matthew 25:8-10*   ▶

. . . the foolish said to the wise, "Give us some of your oil, for our lamps are going out." But the wise answered, saying, "Since there will not be enough for us and for you, go rather to the dealers and buy for yourselves." And while they were going to buy, the bridegroom came . . .

Plowing a field is hard work.

It's even harder if we don't maintain our farm equipment. We can lose days at critical times if we must call in a mechanic.

That's what happens to our opportunities, if we're unprepared. They come and go, like the best days for plowing our fields. We're off taking care of details we've overlooked, while our chance for success slips by.

We must do the extra thing, take the extra class, work the extra hours, volunteer when we don't feel like it, if we want success to be ours. We can't count on someone else to take up the slack, if we want to reach our goal. The responsibility is ours.

— Day 280 —

"Know that the greatest obstacle in your path is none other than yourself."

◄| Luke 21:36 |►

But stay awake at all times, praying that you may have strength to escape all these things that are going to take place, and to stand before the Son of Man.

Some days, sleeping in is all we can think of.

Or going to the lake, or having that extra slice of pizza.

Or we see our dream car drive by, and suddenly our long-term goals don't seem so relevant any longer. Or a pretty girl or handsome guy catches our eye. Who can fight against that?

We want a shot of instant gratification, right now, today.

We can be our own stumbling block. We must be alert and focused on our goal. Otherwise, it will evaporate and be lost forever.

Review your primary objective. Remind yourself why you chose it. List how far you've already come. Recharge your determination. Your goal is still out there. Chase after it!

— Day 281 —

"If you're only going to 'try' to do something, then you've already committed yourself to the eventual failure of reaching your potential."

Proverbs 24:10

◀   ▶

If you faint in the day of adversity, your strength is small.

The story of *The Little Engine That Could* is all about determination during tough endeavors.

The little engine thinks it can, but it expends a great deal of effort to get over the mountain, barely making progress. It's when the engine knows it can be successful that it zips over the pass and races home.

What's our mountain that we only "think" we can get over? It's not going away. For us to be successful, we need to rethink our plan of action. We can't simply *try* to get over the mountain. We must *do* it.

- Launch that website.
- Publish that novel.
- Travel to the other side of the world.

It's your chance to put your success-speak into practice. Life is calling. Decide that you know you can, and get to it.

— Day 282 —

"Time can never be recovered. Once you've lost it, it's gone forever."

Galatians 6:10   ▶

So then, as we have opportunity, let us do good to everyone, and especially to those who are of the household of faith.

Daylight Savings Time starts in March and ends in October. We move the hands of our clock forward, effectively losing an hour of the day.

We moan over the lost time and the things we could have gotten done, but we can't get it back.

It's vanished as though it never was.

Wasted time disappears in much the same way. We lose focus, our plans get waylaid, and we look up to realize we've gotten nothing done.

Our opportunity to prepare for our future is now. Daylight Savings Time doesn't affect our determination to be successful. It doesn't stop us from focusing on our goal.

Focus breeds efficiency, and efficiency breeds our success.

— Day 283 —

"Without forgiveness, there is no future."

◁   *Matthew 6:15*   ▷

*But if you do not forgive others their trespasses, neither will your
Father forgive your trespasses.*

Imagine a tractor-trailer rig traveling down the highway. It
makes a delivery, and it picks up a newly loaded trailer.

It doesn't unhitch the empty one, however. The next time
we see it, the tractor is hauling both trailers. Then three and four
and five. Soon it can no longer manage its way down the
highway, and it becomes stranded on the side of the road.

It seems silly, but that's what unforgiveness is like. We're
pulling around every angry moment, every offense, and every
cruel thing that's happened to us. Over our lifetime, we
accumulate an unwieldy trail of useless anger, and we can no
longer work our way through life.

We become stuck on the side of life's road.

Forgive. Move forward. Your success is waiting on you. It
will only happen when you lighten your load.

— Day 284 —

"Clearing out the logjam in front of you grans you the opportunity to truly shine, to unlock your full potential, to be able to encounter any obstacles and have the ability to not only overcome, but to learn from the encounter."

◀   Isaiah 40:4   ▶

Every valley shall be lifted up, and every mountain and hill be made low; the uneven ground shall become level, and the rough places a plain.

Puerto Rico, after Hurricane Maria in 2017, faced an unusual problem. El Yunque National Forest, the U.S.'s only tropical rain forest, provides 20 percent of the island's fresh water. Not only was downed vegetation an obstacle to accessing that water, the devastated foliage caused mudslides that regularly blocked the roads.

Without the logjams being continually cleared, the full potential of El Yunque's valuable water resource was wasted. It was still there, just unavailable when it was needed.

Life's logjams are the same, blocking us from moving forward toward our goal. We're stuck in a disaster zone, unable to make progress in our plan to access our future success.

It's time to clear the logjams and let our success shine.

— Day 285 —

*"Stepping outside your current situation
will teach you and give greater
understanding of what you are facing."*

◀   Mark 2:12   ▶

*And he rose and immediately picked up his bed and went out
before them all, so that they were all amazed and glorified God,
saying, "We never saw anything like this!"*

A sick man knows only his hospital room.

A lawyer knows the courtroom and books of rules.

A fisherman understands the sea, but not the mountains.

Stepping outside of who we are gives us a new perspective. We can look at things from a different angle and see our situation in a new light.

It's the reason we bring in outside consultants when we face a challenge. He or she can easily see things to which we've become blinded.

When we're overwhelmed with the obstacles blocking our path, step back. Get a fresh viewpoint. We'll soon see a better path to follow.

— Day 286 —

*"Doing something for the wrong reason
and doing something for the right reason
are two different paths to the same goal.
One will reap far greater benefits from
your actions."*

◀ *Matthew 7:13* ▶

*Enter by the narrow gate. For the gate is wide and the way is easy
that leads to destruction, and those who enter by it are many.*

Working a second job isn't at the top of anyone's preferred
list. We miss out on time with family and friends, and it eats into
our leisure schedule.

If we have something to show for our extra effort, something
worthwhile, then we don't mind. If the money runs through our
fingers like water through a sieve, we've wasted our time.

What's your goal?

What's the point of reaching toward your success? Is it to
indulge yourself, or to provide for your child's education fund?
To upgrade to a glamorous car, or to make sure your family has
good transportation?

The money's the same, however we choose to use it. It's the
reason we work for it that makes the difference. Evaluate your
goal. Verify your reasons. Understand your commitment.

— Day 287 —

"There is always a solution to your problem. You just have to find it."

◀   *Psalm 111:10*   ▶

The fear of the LORD is the beginning of wisdom; all those who practice it have a good understanding. His praise endures forever!

Art forgery is a major worldwide problem.

For art that's reputed to come from before 1945, there's an unusual detection method to decide if the work is real or fake.

Nuclear fallout.

The first nuclear tests began in 1945, releasing previously unknown elements into the air, which made their way into plants used to make paint. If we find these in an artwork's paint, it's likely a forgery.

Knowledge is our friend in resolving problems. The more we study and learn, the wider our options.

When you face an obstacle on your path to success, look for solutions. They are there. Be creative. Options always exist.

The only thing holding you back from success is you!

— Day 288 —

"Trying something new is paramount for success."

◀   *2 Corinthians 6:17*   ▶

Therefore go out from their midst, and be separate from them, says the Lord, and touch no unclean thing; then I will welcome you.

Is life working for us?

Are we happy with how things are playing out? The house we live in, the people we're around, or the job we work? Are they helping us find the success we seek?

If we reach a point where we can't find our success in our current situation, then it's time to try something new. As our verse for today says, *Go out, be separate, and live a clean life.*

Then we'll find our success. Our focus on our goal will be clearer, and our path will be straighter. We'll find it easier to push the obstacles out of the way and move past them.

Walt Disney was a newspaper editor fired for lacking imagination and having no good ideas. Look at the success he achieved. We can break out and find our success, when we're unafraid to try something new.

— Day 289 —

*"Refuse to innovate and you'll find that
you've been sitting still while the world
passed you by."*

◀   *Galatians 6:4*   ▶

*But let each one test his own work, and then his reason to boast will
be in himself alone and not in his neighbor.*

Finding success isn't a free ride.

We can't jump onto someone else's cart and make it to our
goal without effort of our own.

Apple was poised for success in the 80s. They missed their
opportunity to enter the business market, and within a decade,
they lost market share to a rival company, bringing Apple to the
brink of bankruptcy.

Their comeback in the late 90s was a result of creative inno-
vation from Apple co-founder Steve Jobs.

What are you going to try differently? Getting more sleep?
Applying for a new position at work? Changing your diet?

Or perhaps writing that book or launching that website? Do
it. Make a plan, learn all about it, and get on the road to success.

— Day 290 —

"If you strive to achieve only what you need, then you are existing only to survive."

◀   *Romans 12:1*   ▶

I appeal to you therefore, brothers, by the mercies of God, to present your bodies as a living sacrifice, holy and acceptable to God, which is your spiritual worship.

It's the chocolate cake that makes life worth living.

We need basic food, both wholesome and nutritious. Water provides us necessary liquids. Yet, life with only daily beans and bread, and only water to drink, gets boring.

Occasionally, we need to indulge in a sweet treat.

Our goal must be our focus, but it can't be our only focus.

What about that occasional dinner on the town? Or a play at the theater? Invite friends over for burgers. Keep it simple, but make it fun. We'll recharge our batteries and be able to double our efforts to reach our goal.

Our success may be in our future, but the path we walk is today. Let's enjoy both.

— Day 291 —

"Do not limit yourself."

◀ Genesis 2:7 ▶

Then the LORD God formed the man of dust from the ground and breathed into his nostrils the breath of life, and the man became a living creature.

What's your impossible thing?

The one that you could never do? Dance on stage? Teach a class of seven-year-olds? Sit through a college lecture with classmates half your age?

Maybe, just maybe, your difficulty lies closer to home. You can't go a day without being on a social media site, or refuse the ice cream or the soap opera or the gossip that comes over the phone.

Our doubts defeat us. God has no such conflicts. He spoke to a man made of dust, and the man became a living creature.

He speaks to us, and he enables us. Our goal becomes closer, our determination is stronger, and we wouldn't dream of not following through. We can envision no limits in God.

— Day 292 —

*"Once you let an opportunity pass you by,
it may be gone forever."*

◀◀   *John 3:5*   ▶▶

*Jesus answered, "Truly, truly, I say to you, unless one is born of
water and the Spirit, he cannot enter the kingdom of God."*

Some opportunities are specific for a time and a place.

A solar eclipse. We can't command it into being. It happens
where and when it happens, and either we avail ourselves of the
opportunity or not.

High school sports. Once we graduate, we can't go back and
be the quarterback. It's too late.

Love. Once it's lost, it never returns in quite the same way.
We're changed, it's changed, and we must build something else.

Our relationship with God is an opportunity too good to
pass up. It's a chance to improve our lives, to upgrade our standard of behavior, and to become like Him.

Choose your goal. Decide on the path you'll walk. Make the
decision today.

— Day 293 —

*"If you are at peace with yourself, you will
be at peace with others."*

◀   *Isaiah 26:3*   ▶

*You keep him in perfect peace whose mind is stayed on you, because
he trusts in you.*

A good start to our morning is a good beginning to our day.

- Lay in bed a few minutes before hopping up.
- Eat breakfast at the table.
- Listen to your favorite song on the way to work.
- Hug someone for a full minute.
- Notice something thoughtful and comment on it.
- Connect with God in a meaningful way.

If we slow down and let peace filter through our thoughts, we'll be softer and kinder to those we meet. We'll think before we speak, consider others' feelings, and respect their opinions.

Our calm behavior will spread. Our connection with God will filter to our acquaintances. We'll return home at night fresher and more relaxed for enjoying our peaceful day. We'll rest better at night, in preparation for another morning.

— Day 294 —

"Seek to understand what you don't know, for knowledge will guide you toward success."

◄ *Proverbs 1:22* ►

How long, O simple ones, will you love being simple? How long will scoffers delight in their scoffing and fools hate knowledge?

For many people, kindergarten is the start of formal education. We're given 13 years until graduation. We're expected to gain what we need to know during that time.

The reality is that 13 years isn't enough. There's college, graduate school, and a doctoral program to complete. We can never slow down.

We're learning all our lives, if not in formal classrooms, then in the daily process of life: how to raise a family, the aspects of growing crops on a farm, or cooperation in the business field.

When we decide to stop learning is when we stop advancing toward our next goal, and there must always be a next goal. We reach one, then move to the next one that's just out of our reach.

What will you learn next? That's what will determine whether you reach your goal.

— Day 295 —

*"To be successful in all aspects of life,
you'll need people's help along the way."*

◀   *Proverbs 19:17*   ▶

*Whoever is generous to the poor lends to the LORD, and he will
repay him for his deed.*

A sapling of a tree will someday be a mighty oak.

Yet when it's young, it can't withstand the onslaught of the wind. It needs to be staked down so that it has the extra strength to stand tall.

When its branches grow broad and reach to the sky, it provides shade to the people who staked it in its youth.

Life is interactive. What we do for others comes back to us. The banker we spoke kindly to will help us with our emergency loan. The gas station attendant will help us fix our flat. Our daughter's daycare teacher will stay late for us when we can't be on time.

When we are generous with our money, our kind words, and our consideration, we'll receive it back in kind, both from the Lord and from the people at our side.

— Day 296 —

"Never compromise on your moral grounds."

◀   *James 4:17*   ▶
So whoever knows the right thing to do and fails to do it, for him it is sin.

An automobile has one primary function: to start every day and get us to where we need to go.

If we get in, and the seats begin to go up and down, then the trunk pops open, and the air conditioner begins to blow, but it doesn't start, the car is useless. If the lights flash on and off, and the wipers wipe, then the sunroof opens, but it won't start, it's no more than a hunk of metal, glass, and plastic.

Our primary function is to maintain our moral center. If we can dance and sing, design a fancy building, or write a novel, but we let our morality be compromised, we're useless.

Our integrity is what compels us toward our goal. It keeps us centered on our path, helps us leap over obstacles (or push them out of the way), and firms up our determination to move forward. When we know the right thing to do *and we do it,* we become a success in all that we attempt.

— Day 297 —

"Stand firm and have unwavering resolve
to make a difference in the world."

◀   *Psalm 51:10*   ▶

Create in me a clean heart, O God, and renew a right spirit within
me.

An office tower must have a firm footing. The taller the building, the deeper the foundations are dug.

When the wind blows, buildings can sway up to several feet. It's enough to make someone seasick.

It's the building's foundation that keeps it from falling over.

Our resolve in the face of our obstacles is what keeps us grounded in our pursuit of our goal. We dig our foundation with preparation, study, and patience. When criticism comes our way, we bend but we don't break.

We close our doors and refuse to let the criticism inside. Our goal is in sight, and we won't turn to the side.

We can only do this when we've scraped all distractions aside. Our foundation is firmly adhered to the bedrock of success.

— Day 298 —

"Listen to the words of the wise, for they often contain great insight."

◀ Proverbs 8:14 ▶

I have counsel and sound wisdom; I have insight; I have strength.

A clown is the entertainment center of the circus. No matter what he does, his actions make us laugh.

His big feet make him stumble.

His red nose is laughable.

He can fit with twelve friends into a tiny car.

We don't take the clown seriously. Even after the show, with the makeup gone, we expect to hear outrageous things from his lips.

We don't ask the clown for investment advice, or counseling over our marriage, or about the color of our living room walls. We don't trust his wisdom because of the part he plays.

Find the wise man, the one who's discovered the path to success. Ask what he thinks. Listen. Take notes. Find out how it's done, and apply his lessons to your life.

— Day 299 —

"If you see somebody in need, don't be afraid to help them."

I waited patiently for the LORD; he inclined to me and heard my cry.

A kitten's first steps are wobbly and unsure.

Yet, the animal will be fleet and limber when she's fully grown. Her mother nudges her gently, licks her fur, and treats her as the treasure she is. The newborn isn't mature yet, but give her time.

The people we interact with are like that kitten. When they stumble, they need time to grow. Through practicing Success-Speak techniques, their legs will soon firm up; they will develop a sense of balance; and they'll become the nimble adult that can walk the dangerous precipice and not slip or fall.

Our job is to nudge them gently, provide them the help they need, and treat them as the treasure they are.

They will soon join us in our journey to success. They will be our support when we're in need, just as we've been theirs.

— Day 300 —

"Learning from a mistake is a success in its own right."

◀   *Proverbs 9:9*   ▶

Give instruction to a wise man, and he will be still wiser; teach a righteous man, and he will increase in learning.

House flipping in California offers heady profits to those with the panache to pull it off.

A husband and wife, displaying their skills before the camera, regularly made snap decisions on their decorating choices. Subway tile here, carpet there, and that kitchen, it must go!

Occasionally, the color scheme on the outside walls wasn't successful, and they repainted a second time at extra expense. During one episode, the husband remarked to his wife, "Remember? We painted that color once before. It didn't work."

Lesson learned, experience taken to heart.

We become wise when our mistakes lift us up rather than pull us down. It's called experience, and we all get to go through it. We can let our lessons trip us up or guide us closer to our success. Stay focused. Our goal is just ahead.

— Day 301 —

"Knowing and understanding the obstacles in your path will enable you to overcome the opposition you face."

◀   Psalm 27:1   ▶

The LORD is my light and my salvation; whom shall I fear?
The LORD is the stronghold of my life; of whom shall I be afraid?

Fear is the goal destroyer.

Mark what that says. The obstacle we face isn't the goal destroyer. The obstruction in our way can be kicked aside, gone over, or skirted around. It's an irritation, but it doesn't preclude us from moving forward.

Our fear of it can.

Once we understand our obstacle, we have a grasp of how to work past it. We see how it's just another thing that we can brush aside, and we can head toward our goal.

The lack of money, a limited education, or the race card, whatever you've been played, make that the element you use as a trampoline to vault forward, always keeping your goal in mind.

Success belongs to the one willing to chase it. It's up to you.

— Day 302 —

"It only takes one step each day to begin
the process of achieving your goals."

◀   Matthew 6:34   ▮▶

Therefore do not be anxious about tomorrow, for tomorrow will be
anxious for itself. Sufficient for the day is its own trouble.

The big picture is sometimes too much.

We stand with our chain saw, and we see two acres that need to be cleared of tall spruce, woody brush, and thick undergrowth.

We can't imagine getting it all done.

We can, though, one tree at a time, one shrub at a time, and one clump of undergrowth at a time. It's the big picture that's unmanageable, not one tree.

Our path to our success can overwhelm us. We see the years of schooling, the practice required, and what we must give up, and we want to throw up our hands before we start.

We're only required to do today. Register for that college course. Lift that weight, the 2 pound one. Resist one dessert for one meal. That's how it starts. Tomorrow can take care of itself.

— Day 303 —

"Just because something seems insurmountable does not mean that it is."

◀ *Psalm 138:3* ▶

On the day I called, you answered me; my strength of soul you increased.

Science can be a solution-giver. Mechanical advantage is a back-saver.

Try to lift something heavy, and we can't do it. Our muscles don't have the strength. Yet attach a series of pulleys, and we lift it with ease.

The pulleys multiply our strength, giving us a mechanical advantage, thanks to science.

Our faith in God and our ability to overcome is our mechanical advantage. He will bring ideas to mind that will act like pulleys, moving us along quicker with less effort than we've expended in the past.

Our job is to trust in Him, to keep moving forward, and to have faith that our goal is within our reach. When we refuse to turn aside, we'll find our success every time.

— Day 304 —

"A mind filled with knowledge is your key to success."

◀ *1 Corinthians 12:8* ▶

For to one is given through the Spirit the utterance of wisdom, and to another the utterance of knowledge according to the same Spirit.

The more we know, the further we go.

Take maps. We're lost without them. Early European explorers made their maps as they went. They drew what they saw, giving those who came after them the opportunity to go a greater distance.

Each explorer added to the knowledge of those before him, and before long, they began to understand where they were headed.

Our success comes to us by filling ourselves with knowledge, one venture at a time. Today we explore a small portion of our plan, and that allows us to move even further afield tomorrow.

Pretty soon, we'll navigate the world and know exactly where we are. Our new levels of knowledge will be our key to reaching our goal.

— Day 305 —

"Selfishness and greed often go hand-in-hand; if you spot one, the other will soon join you."

◄ *James 3:16* ►

For where jealousy and selfish ambition exist, there will be disorder and every vile practice.

Like lines up with like.

It's part of nature. Water runs to water, trees grow on the mountain slopes, and clouds remain in the sky. Dust settles, returning to the soil, and fish remain in the sea.

Kind people tend to be generous; happy people laugh; and selfishness leads to greed.

Placing others first is a learned trait. It doesn't come naturally to us as infants. As children, our lives lead us to share or not, and that follows us into adulthood.

We can change, if we wish. Like lines up with like. If we spend time with generous people, we'll take on a portion of their nature. If we're around selfish people, greed will dig its fingers into every part of who we are. Make the choice. Cast off selfishness. Become a better person. That's finding success.

*"You can either worry . . . or you can trust
God . . . but you CAN'T do both."*

◀ Romans 8:38-39 ▶

*For I am sure that neither death nor life, nor angels nor rulers, nor
things present nor things to come, nor powers, nor height nor depth,
nor anything else in all creation, will be able to separate us from the
love of God in Christ Jesus our Lord.*

Opposites are just that, opposites.

No matter how hard you hit the gas, you can't make your
car go forward and backward at the same time. It simply won't
work. Heat up a steak by placing it in the freezer? No way!

We can't get our house clean while resting on the sofa, either.
We must move to get things done.

Our success is out there. We can see it. It's just beyond our
reach and coming closer. Worrying won't make it happen faster.
Wringing our hands or lying awake at night won't resolve our
perceived issues.

We're started on this path. We can trust in God to take care
of us along the way.

— Day 307 —

"If you want to achieve your goals, to reach out and surpass the impossible; then you must believe that it is not only possible, but that YOU can reach out and succeed."

◀︎   *Matthew 19:26*   ▶︎

But Jesus looked at them and said, "With man this is impossible, but with God all things are possible."

The Hoover Dam is a massive concrete arch-gravity dam in the Black Canyon of the Colorado River.

The project was so massive, people thought it couldn't be built. In 1928, Congress authorized the project, and it was completed two years ahead of time. Six companies banded together using unproven technology to complete the dam. They succeeded because they decided they could.

Your success is in your hands. You make the decisions that lead you forward. Decide on your goal, write up a plan, and then prepare. Study everything you can about your goal. Talk to people in that field. Ask if you can contact them if you have further questions.

This is your time, your day, and your moment. Move forward toward success.

— Day 308 —

"The only way to truly fail is to not even try."

◀   *2 Chronicles 15:7*   ▶

But you, take courage! Do not let your hands be weak, for your work shall be rewarded.

Knowledge comes from experience.

Everything we do provides us knowledge, whether we're successful or not. We might learn how not to do something, or how to perform more successfully in the future.

A pianist might make a mistake at a contest, and for that, he takes a lower score. He vows to improve and practices that passage until he masters it.

He continues to try until he becomes the best he can be.

Everything you try on your path to success won't play out as you intend. You may stumble, or obstacles may block your way. Keep at it. Tomorrow's your chance to try again.

Take a deep breath. Focus on your goal. Don't be overwhelmed. You can move forward.

— Day 309 —

"Wisdom is knowing the time to interfere."

◀   *Proverbs 26:17*   ▶

Whoever meddles in a quarrel not his own is like one who takes a passing dog by the ears.

Dogs are very space-conscious.

They claim their territory, and they don't like to let others slip in. We take our chances when we get too close to an unknown dog. We might get a friendly response, or our fingers might be bloodied.

We take the same chance when we stick our finger in where it doesn't belong. Not everyone wants our advice. It takes wisdom to know when to interfere.

Before you step in, ask yourself how well you know the situation. Are you involved? Does the outcome affect you?

Will the person appreciate your advice?

Help asked for is help appreciated. Unwanted help can bring a snarl.

— Day 310 —

*"Too early or too late and your
opportunity will be gone."*

◀   *Ecclesiastes 3:11*   ▶

*He has made everything beautiful in its time. Also, he has put
eternity into man's heart, yet so that he cannot find out what God
has done from the beginning to the end.*

Microsoft is a massive company today.

When they first entered the stock market, a $10,000 investment would balloon to about $6 million today.

We can't go back and take advantage of that. It was a one-time opportunity. We must move at the right time, or some opportunities are lost.

What opportunities are open for you today?

Education? Register for a class. A new job? Put in your application. Travel? Reserve your seat.

Our opportunities come to us at just the right time. We must be ready. When we're prepared, it's easy to move into our future and find our success.

— Day 311 —

*"You may even feel lost, hopeless, and
completely out of control while your every
achievement and gain is torn from you.
Remember, that's not who you are."*

◀   Psalm 37:23-24   ▶

*The steps of a man are established by the LORD, when he delights
in his way; though he fall, he shall not be cast headlong, for
the LORD upholds his hand.*

In a recent reality show, the CEOs of various companies dressed in an employee's uniform and worked anonymously among low-level employees.

They were unrecognizable in their new position, but it didn't change who they were. Even when they stumbled in their temporary position, they still ran the company and had the power to hire and fire those around them.

We can't let our obstacles determine our self-worth. A job loss doesn't brand us a failure. A broken relationship isn't a stigma, not unless we let it be.

Regroup. Reposition yourself. Go back to the last place you knew your strength, and that's where you start over.

You are who you decide you are. The choice is yours.

— Day 312 —

*"There is still hope. You just need to take
that first step toward rectifying your
problematic situation."*

◀◀   Psalm 145:14   ▶▶

*The LORD upholds all who are falling and raises up all who are
bowed down.*

The worst of situations is just that, a situation. We don't
have to remain in our problem. Here's how to get out:

Get the facts. Proverbs 18:13: *If one gives an answer before he
hears, it is his folly and shame.*

Be open to new ideas. Proverbs 18:15: *An intelligent heart
acquires knowledge, and the ear of the wise seeks knowledge.*

Hear both sides of the story. Proverbs 18:17: *The one who
states his case first seems right, until the other comes and examines
him.*

Take that first step. Use Success-Speak. Don't let anyone say
you can't change what's got you stalled. Remember: all the facts,
new ideas, and hear both sides. You've got this under control, as
soon as you let God have control. He will be your calm assurance
when you let yourself trust in Him.

— Day 313 —

*"Being thankful for the things you have
and the assistance people have offered
will further your path to success."*

◄◄   *2 Corinthians 9:11*   ►►

*You will be enriched in every way to be generous in every way,
which through us will produce thanksgiving to God.*

Teamwork makes reaching our goals easier. We have support when we stumble, and in turn, we are encouraged when we're able to assist those around us.

The team must function together. Here's how it works:

- Understand the goals
- Take reasonable risks
- Be open, honest, and respectful
- Foster a strong sense of belonging
- Practice regular re-examination
- Make decisions together

There will be times we travel alone. Remember to be grateful for where we are and those who have helped us along. We're still a team in many ways, even when we're no longer together. The assistance we've given each other will launch us forward.

— Day 314 —

"Your reach will be unfettered once you overcome your own inhibitions to success."

◄| *2 Corinthians 4:8-9* |►

We are afflicted in every way, but not crushed; perplexed, but not driven to despair; persecuted, but not forsaken; struck down, but not destroyed.

Our most limiting factor is ourselves.

Winston Churchill, the prime minister of Britain during the dark days of WWII, famously said, *"Success is not final; failure is not fatal: It is the courage to continue that counts."*

The United Kingdom rebounded from its brush with calamity to once again become a world power.

Thomas Jefferson, President of the U.S., said, *"I find that the harder I work, the more luck I seem to have."*

Where's our luck? In our hard work. Once we quit saying we *can't*, and we believe we *can*, our future will become clearer. We'll step into tomorrow with success in our feet.

Let's move forward. Our time is now.

— Day 315 —

"Your actions toward success speak louder than your wishful thinking."

◀   *Luke 12:35*   ▶

Stay dressed for action and keep your lamps burning.

Daydreaming is essential . . . up to a point.

We must be able to imagine our goal to achieve it, but there's something to be said for putting our feet into action.

What does the start of your day look like? Are you dressed to take charge of what comes your way?

It won't happen in your comfy pajamas.

Dress for success when you're on the phone. Keep your teeth brushed. Shine your desk. Jot down people's names. Spit out your gum.

Never let trash pile up on the floor.

People will believe you're a success when they see you're a success. Just your words aren't enough.

Be a success at home, and your actions will lead you ahead.

— Day 316 —

*"The actions and the consequences of
those you associate with will reverberate
throughout the lives of everyone near
them."*

◀   Romans 2:5   ▶

*But because of your hard and impenitent heart you are storing
up wrath for yourself on the day of wrath when God's righteous
judgment will be revealed.*

An island isn't alone.

The waves that brush against one shore will affect the water
that flows against another. An island can buffer a distant beach
from an impending hurricane, or it can deflect water back, creat-
ing even further damage.

In 1958 in Lituya Bay in Alaska, a mega-tsunami occurred
when 90 million tons of rock fell into the sea.

What effect are our friends having on us?

Are they deflecting obstructions that hinder us? Or have they
let themselves become the obstruction?

We have a goal. The people we associate with either help us
toward that goal or become obstructions. Let's choose wisely.

— Day 317 —

"Power is relative to the opposition it faces."

◀   *Ephesians 6:11*   ▶

Put on the whole armor of God, that you may be able to stand against the schemes of the devil.

We wear Nomex when we're prepared to battle flames.

Kevlar is our protection from high-velocity impacts.

We choose the defensive clothing that's specially formulated to protect us from what we'll come against.

When we chase success, we must prepare our defenses.

- Have a clear goal
- Write out a plan
- Post it so you'll be reminded
- Study to learn as much as you can
- Celebrate each step you complete

Our preparation is our Nomex and our Kevlar. It's our specially formulated clothing to make us invincible. When we're outfitted for success, our opposition must give way.

— Day 318 —

"Try at least one new thing every single day."

◀   Matthew 7:17-18   ▶*

So, every healthy tree bears good fruit, but the diseased tree bears bad fruit. A healthy tree cannot bear bad fruit, nor can a diseased tree bear good fruit.

A healthy tree needs judicious pruning.

We don't lop all the branches away, just the ones that no longer bear fruit. Flowering shrubs are the same. The buds come from the new growth.

The new growth will produce more results than ever before. We'll have larger, fresher fruit. More blooms will grace our shrubs. We also have to prune away parts of our lives to really bloom; we may need to change our activities to make room for something new.

If we're healthy and moving toward our goal, we won't be the same as yesterday. We'll change, live differently, find refreshed life in our new experiences. What's no longer working needs to be pruned away and cast aside. Only our new growth can be allowed to remain.

— Day 319 —

*"Make the effort to bring your dreams,
your needs, and the goals that extend far
beyond just the necessities into reality."*

◄| Galatians 6:9 |►

*And let us not grow weary of doing good, for in due season we will
reap, if we do not give up.*

The Empire State Building was built at the height of the Great Depression. So was Hoover Dam.

One World Trade Center rose from the devastation of a world-shaking event.

What dream do we have that's too big to achieve?

What disasters do we face that cannot be resolved?

What goal have we set that's simply unreachable?

They are our Empire State Building, our Hoover Dam, and our One World Trade Center. We will rise above our problems, and the world will be amazed at what we've achieved.

Those structures weren't built in a day. Our success will take time. Patience is the key, along with planning, determination, and a willingness to constantly move forward.

— Day 320 —

*"Assist those in need, and that assistance
will be repaid."*

◀   Exodus 17:12   ▶

*But Moses' hands grew weary, so they took a stone and put it under
him, and he sat on it, while Aaron and Hur held up his hands, one
on one side, and the other on the other side. So his hands were
steady until the going down of the sun.*

An old-fashioned barn-raising was a community affair.

Everyone got together, farmers and townfolk, too, and over
a day or a weekend, lifted the frame and put on the roof, so that
one man could have a barn.

In turn, he was expected to do the same for others.

There was no pay, no mortgage, and certainly no favors
earned. It was practicality at its best: helping others who would
one day help in return.

Our path to our goal is played out in a similar way. We help
others surmount their obstacles, and they help us surmount ours.

We can see our goal. Move toward it today.

— Day 321 —

"Success and hard work go hand-in-hand;
it's not something to be achieved easily."

◀   *Proverbs 14:23*   ▶

In all toil there is profit, but mere talk tends only to poverty.

Gardening shows abound on television.

We see blankets of color outside home centers every spring.

In Tyler, Texas, the Rose Capital of America, beautiful gardens are especially appreciated. Each spring, the Tyler Azalea Trail opens the city's backyards to visitors from across the state.

To replicate Tyler's beauty in our own backyard is muscle-intensive work. We must weed, fertilize, and mow. Then do it again and again all spring and summer.

Our reward is lush perennials that come back year after year.

Our success in life takes an equal amount of work. It's an ongoing effort. We can't take a year off and expect our plan to still be in place, as good as ever.

We'll be rewarded according to what we've put into our progress toward our goal.

— Day 322 —

"Action changes lives."

◀   *John 13:17*   ▶

If you know these things, blessed are you if you do them.

A retired fire battalion chief in Pike County, Georgia, knows about action. In 2017, he spotted a violent car crash. The car hit a culvert and flipped end over end. The victim's car was upside down, and the driver wasn't breathing.

The retired chief parked his truck and rendered aid, possibly saving her life.

Action, to be effective, must be timely and decisive.

Too little too late is little better than nothing at all.

If the retired fire chief had finished his errands and returned to help, the woman might not have survived.

When we have a goal, action is our keyword. We might be researching how to proceed or meeting with experts for advice. We may find ourselves pounding the pavement to look for job opportunities. Getting off our sofa will help us toward our goal.

— Day 323 —

*"There is a difference between dreaming
of a better life and living it."*

◄| *Proverbs 21:21* |►

*Whoever pursues righteousness and kindness will find life,
righteousness, and honor.*

John Paul DeJoria sold Christmas cards before he was 10 to support his family. Today, his John Paul Mitchell Systems brings in millions of dollars annually.

Ursula Burns was raised in a housing project. She rose to head Xerox, becoming CEO and chairwoman.

Leonardo Del Vecchio grew up in an orphanage and began producing Ray-Bans and Oakley sunglasses. His estimated worth in 2011 was $10 billion dollars.

There's a reason we hear so may rags-to-riches stories. When we have very little, we're motivated to do whatever it takes to find success.

What's your success goal? It's out there waiting on you, but you must take the first step. Plan. Study. Decide to act. Your success will come only as quickly as you pursue it.

— Day 324 —

"If there are multiple paths to the same goal, choose the one that is correct for your skillset."

◀   *Exodus 36:2*   ▮▶

And Moses called Bezalel and Oholiab and every craftsman in whose mind the LORD had put skill, everyone whose heart stirred him up to come to do the work.

People's differences are what give us our strength.

What one person struggles with, another can step in and do easily. Computer skills come easily to some, and others enjoy working with their hands in the dirt.

It's when we are heading down a career path we don't enjoy that we'll struggle with our motivation to move forward.

Think about what you're good at. What's brought you success in the past? Research how you can use that skill.

What path to your goal does that open?

Our plan for our future is a very individual one. What works for one person may not work for another. Find out the facts. See what works. Choose and move ahead.

— Day 325 —

*"Do what's right even when you don't have
to. It will change your life for the better."*

◄   I Thessalonians 5:15   ►

*See that no one repays anyone evil for evil, but always seek to do
good to one another and to everyone.*

When you take your car in for an oil change, the technician doesn't have to check your tires.

When they do, it may prevent you getting a flat, and it also motivates you to return next time.

Not only do you get reassurance from the exchange, the person who helped you receives the promise of continued business.

It's a matter of gratitude. Kind deeds and doing what's right help improve our attitude, and we inspire motivation in those around us.

When we do what's right even when we don't have to, we empower the person we've helped, but we also empower ourselves.

— Day 326 —

"Giving your best when you don't feel like it motivates others to do the same."

◀   Romans 5:8   ▶

But God shows his love for us in that while we were still sinners, Christ died for us.

A smile goes a long way.

So does a candy bar or a cup of coffee, one that's given when it's least expected.

It's why we have secret Santas at Christmas. Even when we're tired and ready for the day to end, we still get a pleased response from those we've given the gift.

It's even better because they don't know who to thank. The happiness begins to spread, and the excitement grows.

It works in all areas of our life. Greet someone with a smile. Hold the door. Offer to carry a package. Include their errand with yours. Encourage them with a Success-Speak quote.

Do it with a pleasant word even when you don't feel like it, and your positive attitude will begin to spread.

— Day 327 —

*"How successful you've been isn't
measured by where you are in life but
instead by how far you've come."*

◄   *Job 17:9*   ►

*Yet the righteous holds to his way, and he who has clean hands
grows stronger and stronger.*

The tallest buildings in the world are measured differently. Do we count the height from the lowest basement, from ground level, or how far it is above sea level?

Mountains are the same. Mount Everest reaches highest above sea level, but Mauna Kea in Hawaii is taller when measured from base to summit.

Do you want to measure your success by someone else's "sea level," or from where you started?

Rags to riches is a much more impressive success story than riches to riches, even if the second has more cash in the bank. That's why our culture is taken with self-made men. They've come from nothing to having everything they dreamed.

What's your success story going to look like? Family gathered around? A beach house? Owning a jet plane? It's your choice.

— Day 328 —

"Have faith and perseverance in pursuit of the success you are truly capable of achieving!"

◀ *Revelation 2:10* ▶

Do not fear what you are about to suffer. Behold, the devil is about to throw some of you into prison, that you may be tested, and for ten days you will have tribulation. Be faithful unto death, and I will give you the crown of life.

Success is often difficult.

Nelson Mandela spent 27 years in prison before successfully being elected president of South Africa.

Mahatma Gandhi was assassinated for his success.

Donald Trump was vilified by many politicians after being elected president.

What price are we willing to pay for success? Four years of college? Risking our rent on an investment opportunity? Spending our vacation time pursuing new options for reaching our goal?

We will suffer for our success. Be prepared, then go for it!

— Day 329 —

"If you are embarrassed to stand by what
you've done, a change is in order."

◀ *Genesis 3:10* ▶

And [Adam] said, "I heard the sound of you in the garden, and I
was afraid, because I was naked, and I hid myself."

When we strip away the coverings, what's revealed?

Who are we? What will people see?

- ✓ Kindness?
- ✓ Generosity?
- ✓ The likeness of our heavenly Father?

If we can check these off, we're in pretty good shape. What about the rest of us?

Do we flip the computer monitor off when someone peers over our shoulder? Do we mute the television when the pastor calls? Does the wine on the dinner table present an issue for church members we invite for Sunday lunch?

If we hear the sound of Jesus coming up beside us, what behaviors will we change? That's how we should live now.

— Day 330 —

"If it doesn't challenge you, it won't change you."

◀ Amos 5:14-15 ▶

*Seek good, and not evil, that you may live; and so the LORD, the
God of hosts, will be with you, as you have said. Hate evil, and love
good, and establish justice in the gate; it may be that the LORD, the
God of hosts, will be gracious to the remnant of Joseph.*

The Iditarod, the iconic sled dog race through Alaska, origi-
nates in Settler's Bay and concludes in Nome.

It's a life-changing feat for those who complete the trip.

The Ironman World Championship held in Hawaii involves
swimming, biking, and running. It's considered by many to be
the most difficult sports challenge on the planet. Some people
enter knowing they have no chance of winning. It's the experience they're after. They say it changes them.

Your goal is only a challenge if it will change who you are. If
reaching it is easy, and you're the same person when it's over,
you've wasted your time. Think big. Find your challenge. Make
your life count.

— Day 331 —

"Opportunities will come knocking on
your door many times during your life,
but if you don't greet and utilize them,
success will not be yours."

◀| *Colossians 4:5* |▶

Walk in wisdom toward outsiders, making the best use of the time.

There are four ways to look at wisdom.

- It can be accumulated learning, either scientific or philosophical.
- It might be the ability to discern things not obvious to the untaught, using our insight.
- Wisdom can simply be using good sense.
- It's also an accepted although unproven belief generally held by historians or scientists.

These reveal four ways we can hear opportunity knocking at our door. We can rely on what we've been taught, take advantage of what just jumps out at us, fall back on our good sense, or ask others what they would do.

The ultimate responsibility falls back on us. We must be aware of what's around us, reach out when opportunity comes our way, and never look back or consider giving up.

— Day 332 —

"Overcome all that stands in your path, achieve success, and live a life that is honorable and true."

◀   Proverbs 14:31   ▶

Whoever oppresses a poor man insults his Maker, but he who is generous to the needy honors him.

Not many people hold up tyrants as role models.

Drug lords, either. They've achieved a broken sort of success, but it's not the path we want our children to take. They've become rich through taking advantage of the poor.

That's not okay. Proverbs 14:31 says we insult God when we walk on people to reach our goal.

It's the generous person who's lived a life that's honorable and true.

Mother Teresa, by her testament, owned only a single sari to her name. Mahatma Gandhi had a net worth of $1,000. Both were rich in success, because they walked paths that were honorable and true.

What's your goal? Make sure your path honors the needy.

— Day 333 —

"Admirable goals are worth the work to accomplish."

◀   *Jeremiah 17:7*   ▶

Blessed is the man who trusts in the LORD, whose trust is the LORD.

We share the Nobel Prize for the most admirable accomplishments in the world, from literature, physics, and chemistry, to peace, economics, and physiology/medicine.

It's a level of award that makes people stand up and notice. They say, "Wow," and are amazed.

Will our goal do that? Will people look back on our life and say we were wonders to accomplish what we did?

- Harriet Tubman saved 300 slaves on the Underground Railroad.
- Irena Sendler smuggled 400 babies out of Nazi Germany.
- Oskar Schindler spent his fortune to save 1100 Jews from Auschwitz.

Our goal needs to make others take notice. Will yours?

— Day 334 —

"Stepping back will give perspective and a superior understanding of what has happened and of what is to come, allowing you to make purposeful decisions."

◀︎   Genesis 50:20   ▶︎

As for you, you meant evil against me, but God meant it for good, to bring it about that many people should be kept alive, as they are today.

Joseph, in the Old Testament, was an outstanding man.

He displayed honesty, respect, and dependability as an adult.

Yet, he was continually beat down. Eventually, he rose to power in Egypt, and at the height of his authority, he looked back and saw what was invisible to him earlier.

God had taken what his brothers meant for evil—selling him into slavery—and turned it to good. His interpretation of the pharaoh's dream enabled him to save a nation in time of drought, and bring his family to the best lands in Egypt.

Our best decisions come from the knowledge we've gained.

Step back, think about where you are, and decide where you want to go. Your future is waiting on you. Choose wisely.

— Day 335 —

"The ruler of success measures our
progress from our start point, not from
our present location."

◀︎   Proverbs 4:18   ▶︎
But the path of the righteous is like the light of dawn, which shines
brighter and brighter until full day.

The sun is constantly in motion.

So is the earth, traveling at 67,000 miles per hour on its trip around our star.

The earth rotates at the equator at 1,000 miles per hour.

Our clocks keep time 24 hours a day, yet we measure our activities from dawn, from the breaking of the sun, from sunrise to sunset. That's what really counts to us, and it's the reason for Daylight Savings Time. We want to make the most of our day.

It's the point from where we measure that determines what we've accomplished.

Our success is measured from our starting point. Yours isn't the same as anyone else's. Use your ruler, measure your distance, and if you're moving forward, celebrate how far you've come.

— Day 336 —

*"Just because you've set a goal to achieve
doesn't mean it will come easily."*

1 Chronicles 4:10 ▶

*Jabez called upon the God of Israel, saying, "Oh that you would
bless me and enlarge my border, and that your hand might be with
me, and that you would keep me from harm so that it might not
bring me pain!" And God granted what he asked.*

Pain is something to be avoided.

A hot stove, a broken relationship, or a failed financial trans-
action can be difficult to live with.

Yet there are benefits to our pain. It sets out our parameters.
If we touch that, it will hurt. Doing something else will boom-
erang on us. We'd better use wisdom in our next investment.

We learn to use improved judgment when making decisions.

Working hard and enduring suffering to reach our goal
makes it sweeter when it comes. We know the price we paid, and
we treasure our success more for it. Jabez's name meant "pain,"
and he overcame that. We can overcome our struggles and reach
our goal.

— Day 337 —

"In the face of losing everything, you learn what's important in your life."

◀ Luke 15:22-24 ▶

But the father said to his servants, "Bring quickly the best robe, and put it on him, and put a ring on his hand, and shoes on his feet. And bring the fattened calf and kill it, and let us eat and celebrate. For this my son was dead, and is alive again; he was lost, and is found." And they began to celebrate.

Other people won't understand our response to our loss.

In the story of The Prodigal Son, the younger brother was incensed that his father treated his elder brother royally when he returned from his foray into independence and debauchery.

The father only knew his excitement at his errant son's return.

As we pursue our goal, our journey will come with costs. Life does that to us. Our challenge is to take our mind off what we give up and focus on what we gain.

What's lost doesn't define us. What we learn and the progress we make does.

— Day 338 —

"The word 'impossible' is just an excuse to not achieve success."

◀ Judges 6:15 ▶

And he said to him, "Please, Lord, how can I save Israel? Behold, my clan is the weakest in Manasseh, and I am the least in my father's house."

We know the story of Gideon and the fleece he set out before God. Then, to be certain, he repeated it the following night.

Gideon was a man of valor and bravery in the face of an opposing and terrifying opponent. He brought down his enemy.

Yet, he tried to beg off his brightest moment with a weak excuse. God would have none of it, assuring Gideon his power came from God, not from his standing in the clans of Israel.

What's our weak excuse?

Why are we not making progress toward our goal?

Our strength comes from our faith in God, our preparation for our future, and our determination to move forward no matter how daunting the journey seems. Our path awaits. Let's go.

— Day 339 —

"Fear can't be your focus. You need to overcome your fear and not let it hinder your progress in life."

4I   Isaiah 43:1   I▶

But now thus says the LORD, he who created you, O Jacob, he who formed you, O Israel: "Fear not, for I have redeemed you; I have called you by name, you are mine."

Warren Buffett, one of the richest people on the planet, spent his college years avoiding classes that forced him to stand and speak in class.

Joel Osteen gave his first sermon at 36 and recalls being "scared to death."

Mahatma Gandhi suffered frequent panic attacks and on one occasion in London read one line from his speech and had to let someone else take over.

You can move past your fear into your success.

Thomas Jefferson and Abraham Lincoln were terrified of facing large crowds. Look what they managed to achieve.

Overcome your fear. Move out. Make progress. Find success.

— Day 340 —

"Complete success can be achieved only by being accountable for your actions."

◄ *Proverbs 28:13* ►

Whoever conceals his transgressions will not prosper, but he who confesses and forsakes them will obtain mercy.

Charles Ponzi built a financial empire in the early years of the 20th century conning investors into sending him money.

This type of fraud is still known as a Ponzi scam.

P.T. Barnum touted one attraction in his traveling show as George Washington's 161-year-old nurse. Her later autopsy proved her to be no more than 80.

Barnum also printed his own obituary, so he could read it before he died, proving himself the king of the hucksters.

Your true success comes in being on the face of things what you are at your core. When people see behind your façade, will they like what they find?

If you make a mistake, be open about it. Own up to your flaws, change who you are, and become better than you were.

— Day 341 —

"Until you have been brought low, you can never truly appreciate what it is to be raised high."

◀ *Psalm 57:1* ▶

Be merciful to me, O God, be merciful to me, for in you my soul takes refuge; in the shadow of your wings I will take refuge, till the storms of destruction pass by.

Our background is our status quo. We don't see what we've grown up with as special or outstanding, no matter how luxurious our lifestyle. It only seems extravagant or special to those who don't have it.

The Twin Towers in New York were of little note for most people, until they were destroyed.

People rode a wave of easy credit until the financial crisis of 2008, when subprime mortgages crippled the housing market.

Your success is more than money. It comes in your family, your friends, and in safe housing; in having enough food to eat; and in trusting in God for your future.

If those are gone, your success will feel hollow. Treasure them as part of your path. They will enrich your journey.

— Day 342 —

"You have the gift of choice. You must choose to live a life of success."

◂ Psalm 16:8 ▸

I have set the LORD always before me; because he is at my right hand, I shall not be shaken.

The traffic light turns from green to red.

We apply the brakes as we see the lane markings on the road. We're forced to choose, either right or left.

Before our car is in motion again, our decision is cast. Our lane has been selected, and we no longer have the opportunity to change to the right or to the left.

Whichever direction we choose, we can be assured our Lord has it covered. When we're sick, he's our healer. When we're in need, he's our financial advisor.

The choice is ours. As we travel through life, we can set our goal to achieve success. Either left or right, the road we travel reflects the decisions we've made.

Success must be our goal. How we achieve it is up to us.

— Day 343 —

"Want to know what's most important to you in life? Take a hard look at what you spend the majority of your time doing."

Matthew 6:21   ▶

For where your treasure is, there will your heart be also.

Here's a simple evaluation you can do to determine your passions and goals.

For one week, carry a notepad with you and write down the different activities you do. Mark the time they start and stop.

At the end of the week, take 30 minutes and list the activities. Underline the ones you do for others. Circle the ones you do for yourself.

Then total the minutes you spent doing each one.

If you have a greater number of underlined activities, you're a giver. Do circles rule? You like to make time for yourself.

Order your activities by the minutes spent on each one, and you'll know your passion. It doesn't matter what you say you enjoy, if you're not making time for it, it's not driving your life.

Having passion drives you. What's yours? That's your goal.

— Day 344 —

"If you find achieving your goal is becoming difficult, DON'T STOP! It just means you are moving closer to the summit of success!"

1 Peter 5:8-9   ▶

Be sober-minded; be watchful. Your adversary the devil prowls around like a roaring lion, seeking someone to devour. Resist him, firm in your faith, knowing that the same kinds of suffering are being experienced by your brotherhood throughout the world.

Top athletes have a secret to their success.

They increase their performance by damaging their bodies.

You read that right. Each time they work out beyond their comfort zone, they create micro-tears in their muscle tissue. As it heals, the tiny bits of scar tissue make the muscle stronger than it was before.

That's exactly how it is when we step out toward our goal. It can be tough. No one's denying that. Each strain or setback creates micro-tears in our dedication. It hurts. Yet, as these micro-tears heal themselves, the scar tissue that remains is our strongest point.

Don't stop! Success-Speak works! Keep achieving today!

— Day 345 —

*"There are no perfect conditions, only
perfect opportunities."*

◀ *2 Corinthians 1:9* ▶

*Indeed, we felt we had received the sentence of death. But this
happened that we might not rely on ourselves but on God, who
raises the dead.*

No one has a perfect life.

We make our opportunities where we are. We take the conditions of our lives, and we find the nuggets of opportunity in the everyday moments.

A poor grade on our college finals? We make faith our firm footing.

A difficult spouse? We find a greater wellspring of love.

A miscarriage? We discover compassion for others' children.

Cancer? This is a hard one. We show our loved ones Jesus is there for them.

These goals will hit close to the core of who we are. They reveal the reality of life. Choose carefully for success.

— Day 346 —

"You have not failed unless you give up. Continue onward . . . persist . . . don't stop . . . for your success may be around the next corner."

◀   *Philippians 1:6*   ▶

And I am sure of this, that he who began a good work in you will bring it to completion at the day of Jesus Christ.

The intrepid carpenter who decides to build his own house has quite a chore in front of him. There's foundation work, plumbing to install, and walls to frame.

Then there's the roof, windows, insulation, and electrical; and he's not even to the finish work.

Here's what makes his endeavor a success. He's got a vested interest in what he's building. It's his money, his time, and his effort. To walk away is to abandon his investment. Just because the trim's incomplete doesn't mean he's willing to give up.

He'll keep at the construction until it's a success.

The goal you've selected is the same as that house. You have a vested interest through your money, your time, and your effort. To abandon it is to abandon your investment. Keep focused on your goal. Once you finish the basics, the rest is trim work.

— Day 347 —

"Something is impossible only as long as you believe it cannot be done."

◀   *Mark 11:24*   ▶

Therefore I tell you, whatever you ask in prayer, believe that you have received it, and it will be yours.

Larry Ellison was born in New York on the Lower East Side.

After he contracted pneumonia as a baby, he was adopted by his great-aunt and great-uncle and lived on the South Side of Chicago.

Ellison never met his birth father.

He moved from a poor beginning to co-founding Oracle and eventually owning an entire Hawaiian island.

There's no leap too big for you to make.

You're limited only by how big you can dream.

You need milestones along the way that you can mark off, but you need a goal big enough to test your faith. Imagine it. Plan for it. Act on it. Your future is what you can imagine, what you work for, and what you give your best to.

— Day 348 —

*"The greatest success in life is
accomplishing the will of God."*

◀   *1 Peter 3:17*   ▶

*For it is better to suffer for doing good, if that should be God's will,
than for doing evil.*

Our purpose in life is to become better than we were. We
must be renewed after the image of the Creator.

The process involves stepping back from our daily life and
seeing how we're living in light of the Bible. We can perform a
test to determine the will of God.

We ask ourselves what it good and acceptable and perfect.
We immerse ourselves in the written Word of God. We saturate
our minds with it. Then we model ourselves after the qualities we
discover there.

Now we have a good basis for selecting our goal in life. We
have a better understanding of what we need in order to experience true success. We know the direction of our success, and we
can aim our arrow that way.

The good that flows from God is our best guide to success.

— Day 349 —

"Climbing a mountain is often hardest just before you reach the peak. You're nearly there!"

◄ Micah 4:1 ►

It shall come to pass in the latter days that the mountain of the house of the LORD shall be established as the highest of the mountains, and it shall be lifted up above the hills; and peoples shall flow to it.

Mountain climbing challenges us in two ways.

1. The sheer effort of lifting our body weight step after step is exhausting.
2. The air becomes thinner, and our bodies cannot get enough oxygen.

The higher we go, the more pronounced these issues will become, until many people give up and refuse to go higher.

When we're exhausted is when we're closest to the top. Our goal is just through the mist. We need to lift our feet one more time. Take one more breath. Determine we've come too far to turn around now.

When we're ready to go the distance, our goal will be ours.

— Day 350 —

*"A lack of interest is to failure, as
perseverance is to success."*

◀   Isaiah 40:28-29   ▶

*Have you not known? Have you not heard? The LORD is the
everlasting God, the Creator of the ends of the earth. He does not
faint or grow weary; his understanding is unsearchable. He gives
power to the faint, and to him who has no might he increases
strength.*

Many reasons can steal our interest and our motivation from
us. We must reach out to regain what we've lost.

1. God will comfort us when we're discouraged.
2. We can trust Him for hope when we're lost in our pain.
3. He'll empower us when we are bogged down.
4. In Him, our indifference will change to joy.

We might need to rearrange the furniture, call an old friend,
or try out a hobby from when we were a teen. Perhaps a weekend
away will provide the spark we need. Attend church. See a movie.
Volunteer in your goal's field.

Your goal hasn't evaporated. Be persistent. It's still out there.

— Day 351 —

"Kind words said today create
opportunities for tomorrow."

◀ *Proverbs 15:4* ▶

A gentle tongue is a tree of life, but perverseness in it breaks the
spirit.

Remember your schoolyard days.

Which do you recall most clearly, the nice words said or the ones that cut you?

You probably remember who said them, too.

As an adult, who would you be most likely to partner with in business?

People have good memories, and what's said sticks with them. Kind words make a difference.

When we treat people well, we create a positive relationship that can open doors later in life.

Be kind. Be positive. Create opportunities for yourself.

Your future success might depend on it.

— Day 352 —

"The rocks in our way can become
building blocks for our future."

◀   Isaiah 41:13   ▶

For I, the LORD your God, hold your right hand; it is I who say to
you, "Fear not, I am the one who helps you."

In America's New England states, many early farmers fought with rocky soil.

They could have given up and found more fertile land. Instead, they dug out the rocks and made rubble fences out of them. Many of their fences still divide the landscape today.

Our obstacles are sometimes the best things for us. They teach us lessons, provide us time to ponder our next step, and instill in us a fresh sense of purpose.

Bill Gates' first company, Traf-O-Data, failed miserably. The failed design was pivotal in developing Microsoft's initial products several years later.

Having patience and perseverance is vital on the path to success. Forget either one, and we risk giving up too soon. Use your failures to create a new foundation for your success.

— Day 353 —

"Stand straight, stand tall, don't fear those that would challenge you."

◀︎   Psalm 118:6   ▶︎

The LORD is on my side; I will not fear. What can man do to me?

Three of the top four fears we endure include ridicule, rejection, and death.

All are valid to the sufferer. We're afraid of not projecting a good image, that we might mess up and get a negative response. We blindly follow the crowd become others' acceptance of us is essential to our self-worth. We shudder at the thought of the unknown. What's our future? Heaven, hell?

The top fear we endure is failure. Our actions are wrapped up in avoiding it. Not succeeding in our plans, hitting rock bottom, or not meeting this week's quota at work can trigger our fear.

Failing is subjective and personal. It isn't on the same level for everyone. Our only true failure is to run away when we're bullied or challenged. We must stick to our plan, continue to pursue our goal, and be confident in our eventual success.

— Day 354 —

"The people to look up to are those who are already successful."

◄| *Proverbs 13:20* |►

Whoever walks with the wise becomes wise, but the companion of fools will suffer harm.

The field of medicine requires three to five years of residency training after finishing our university work. The internship can run to seven years in intensive fields, like neurosurgery.

Why? We learn from successful people. We watch them, see how it's done, and put the skills into practice in a success-producing manner.

We might get advice from a master gardener, watch training videos over computer skills, or take a class at a home center to learn to replace a broken window.

We're learning from people who are *good at doing things.* Maybe we've watched our parents and think they've done a good job. Or our pastor or Sunday school teacher. Maybe it's the owner of the coffee shop we visit.

When we see success in others, that's what we should admire.

— Day 355 —

"What are you afraid of? Someone has already conquered it. You can do it, too!"

Little by little I will drive them out from before you, until you have increased and possess the land.

Everyone does things for the first time. Everyone.

Pick a successful person. At one time he or she was fourteen and tentative about life. They had to be courageous, step out into a world that didn't pat them on the back, and make their way just like everyone else.

They did it one successful decision at a time.

What's your fear? A challenge to your ethnic background? Your education? Your gender? A fear that having a family will hold you back, or that not having one will do the same?

Successful people have moved forward despite all these challenges. It's not the challenge that matters most. It our determination to get past it.

Success is infused with fortitude. It drives us forward.

— Day 356 —

"When you stumble, check to see if the
object in your way looks like you."

◀◀   *1 Samuel 16:7*   ▶▶

But the LORD said to Samuel, "Do not look on his appearance or
on the height of his stature, . . . for the LORD sees not as man sees:
man looks on the outward appearance, but the LORD looks on the
heart."

There are six basic steps to success.

- Identify your goal.
- Study to see what it takes.
- Write down a plan.
- Act on that plan daily.
- Be patient with the pacing of your progress.
- Let determination be your motivator.

When you feel you're not making progress, review this list.
See if any of these have been overlooked or ignored. Are you still
doing something every day toward your goal?

Don't let your patience wear thin. Frustration can't be per-
mitted. Step forward. Continue to move ahead.

— Day 357 —

*"Sometimes people won't hear your voice
because of the things you do."*

◀| *1 John 3:18* |▶

Little children, let us not love in word or talk but in deed and in truth.

See if this sounds familiar:

"Do as I say, not as I do."

We've all heard it, and we know it doesn't work. People emulate actions, not words.

Our example to others comes in our behavior. They see our responses to stressful situations, how we react to challenges, and what causes us to lose our cool.

When we think we're portraying success, we're revealing an incomplete picture if we leave out concern, empathy, and consideration.

The people around us are an important part of reaching our goal. If we carelessly cast them aside to get ahead, our success will be shallow and unfulfilling.

— Day 358 —

"Preparation is your decision to become successful."

◀ *Ezekiel 38:7* ▶

Be ready and keep ready, you and all your hosts that are assembled about you, and be a guard for them.

We can plan an elaborate trip to a major theme park, even get the kids all excited, but if we don't buy the airline tickets and reserve our hotel room, it's not happening. We can't wake up on the day of our departure and decide we're taking care of it then.

It's all empty and wishful thinking if we don't prepare for the actual trip.

Success is the same. Know your goal. Write out your plan. Act on it.

How do you know the steps to take to move forward?

Subscribe to magazines in your intended field. Take a college class. Contact successful experts. Maintain open communication with people who can give you assistance.

Do what it takes.

— Day 359 —

"Each tick of the clock is a second of your life gone. Get busy now!"

◀   *2 Corinthians 6:2*   ▶

For he says, "In a favorable time I listened to you, and in a day of
salvation I have helped you." Behold, now is the favorable time;
behold, now is the day of salvation.

From the standpoint of youth, life is forever. We can't imagine the end of it.

As we mature, we see the timeframes shrink. Will we work long enough to pay off that mortgage? Can we afford to invest for years and wait on a return?

When we near retirement, things become imperative. The clock is ticking away.

Whatever stage we're at, we should have goals. We're not reaching them yesterday. Life moves on. If we're not grasping our opportunities today, they are slipping farther away.

Now is the favorable time to reach for our goal. Now is our moment to start toward our success. Now is the opportunity to make our dream come true.

— Day 360 —

*"How you fill your day tells what you want
out of your life."*

◀   ◀   *1 Timothy 6:18-19*   ▮▶

*They are to do good, to be rich in good works, to be generous
and ready to share, thus storing up treasure for themselves as a good
foundation for the future, so that they may take hold of that which
is truly life.*

Stagnation or transformation . . .

One is unpleasant and not beneficial to anyone. The other is
bright, new, and uplifting.

Which life do we live?

Our verse in Timothy says *to do good . . . be rich in good works
. . . generous . . . and ready to share.*

Timothy says one more thing. When we do these things, we
take hold of that which is truly life.

What's your day been like so far? What have you done that's
generous? Have you shared your Success-Speak quote today?

How we fill our day tells the world who we are inside.

— Day 361 —

*"If your goal isn't out of your comfort
zone, you need to think bigger."*

◀   Matthew 16:24   ▶

*Then Jesus told his disciples, "If anyone would come after me, let
him deny himself and take up his cross and follow me."*

Our comfort zone is where we feel safe.

No one can harm us, and if we get poor feedback from the
world, we can withdraw into our safe space and be protected.

That doesn't get us any closer to our goal and to success.

The world isn't going to knock on our door and say, "We've
been watching you, and we think you're primed for success.
Here's the key to the corner office."

We must do what we don't feel safe doing, if we're to pursue
our goals. That means we spend time on the phone calling perspective clients. We manage babysitters and bus schedules.

Getting outside of our comfort zone might be getting out of
our pajamas each morning. Do it! Put on your business face and
make your way onto the path to your success.

— Day 362 —

*"Yesterday is a closed door. Look forward
to find today's success."*

◀   *Genesis 19:26*   ▶

*But Lot's wife, behind him, looked back, and she became a pillar of
salt.*

Time is linear. It runs like a line along a beach from yesterday
to today to tomorrow.

Yesterday is etched in the sand, today is still being drawn,
and tomorrow is an empty stretch of pristine shore.

At the end of our days, the tides of life will smooth the sand
for another generation.

We can't undo yesterday. We can only control the line being
drawn today. Tomorrow hasn't happened and may not be ours.

If we spend our time looking where we've been, we'll not be
able to direct our line today.

Success is somewhere in front of us. The line on the beach
isn't complete. Its future is in our hands.

We choose the direction we travel. Move toward success.

— Day 363 —

"Look in the mirror to find your problem solver. It's up to you to change what you don't like."

◀ Psalm 50:15 ▶

And call upon me in the day of trouble; I will deliver you, and you shall glorify me.

We are more capable than we think.

We often don't realize it, because we've trusted in others to handle our problems, and now it's our turn.

We can't let our fears rob us of our chance for success. We can't spend time protecting our feelings only to lose our opportunity to overcome our problems.

We're like a butterfly struggling to get out of its cocoon. We must do it on our own. If someone tries to make our way easier, we won't be ready, and we'll never fly.

No one knows what's best for us. We don't know what's best for others. The truth is that we must have faith in our preparation for our future success, and we must exhibit the confidence to step out on our path. It's out there waiting on us. Change what it takes to move forward and aim toward your goal.

— Day 364 —

"Put both hands on the handlebars. It's the only way to stay out of the ditch."

◀◀ Titus 2:11-12 ▶▶

For the grace of God has appeared, bringing salvation for all people, training us to renounce ungodliness and worldly passions, and to live self-controlled, upright, and godly lives in the present age,

Schoolboys love to show off their prowess on their bikes. Riding hands-in-the-air is great, until the bike begins to swerve.

The path to success is like a narrow bridge, one with no guardrails and a steep drop-off on each side.

Each edge is brightly painted with directional signals and posted with warning signs, telling how to keep moving along.

- Renounce atrocious behaviors!
- Maintain high standards!
- Respect other people!

These are our markers to find success. Ignore them, and we risk falling off the edge. We'll be safe as long as our hands are on the handlebars, and we keep success in our sights.

— Day 365 —

*"If your year hasn't been successful, what
are YOU going to do about it?"*

◀| *Ephesians 1:11* |▶

*In him we have obtained an inheritance, . . . according to the
purpose of him who works all things according to the counsel of his
will.*

Our lives are a smorgasbord of possibilities. We can reach out and choose anything we want.

Of course, no choice comes without a price. Perhaps we want security most of all. Or to run our own business, or simply to be good at the job we do.

Success is different to everyone. The point is, have you achieved yours? If not, why?

The small steps we complete on our way to our goal are just as much a measure of success as our ultimate achievement. Often, they are more satisfying, because they bring us closer to our destination.

Moving forward gives us purpose and fulfills us emotionally. Keep on your journey. Nothing can hold you back.

Scripture References in
Success-Speak, Annotated Edition.

www.ingramcontent.com/pod-product-compliance
Lightning Source LLC
Chambersburg PA
CBHW060239100426
42742CB00011B/1579